SET ME FREE
A Journey Toward Self-Freedom

SET ME FREE

A Journey Toward Self-Freedom
-Stories-

April Y. Jones

The names and identifying characteristics of many of the individuals featured throughout this book have been changed to protect their privacy. In some cases, composite characters have been created or timelines have been compressed, in order to further preserve privacy and to maintain narrative flow. The goal in all cases was to protect people's privacy without damaging the integrity of the story.

Set Me Free. Copyright © 2023 by April Y. Jones. All rights reserved. Printed in the United States of America. No part of this book may be used or reproduced in any manner whatsoever without written permission except in the case of brief quotations embodied in critical articles and reviews.

Scriptures marked KJV are taken from the King James Version (KJV): King James Version, public domain.

This book may be purchased for educational, business or sales promotional use. For information, please email the author at ajonesmft@aprilyjonestherapy.com.

First Edition

Library of Congress Control Number: 2023908350

IBSN 978-1-7370485-6-5 (Hardcover)
IBSN 978-1-7370485-7-2 (Paperback)

This book is dedicated to everyone who has had to figure out life, to those who are still figuring out life and for those who will have to figure out life again after they once had it all figured out. To those who are striving to be set free from not only others but themselves. Those who have been set free in any area of their life and from anything that was holding on to them or that they were holding on to that caused chaos and robbed them of peace. Remember that you do not have to have it all figured out all at once and all the time. One step at a time, one second at a time. Be free.

Contents

INTRODUCTION	1
1 YOU CAN RUN BUT CAN YOU HIDE?	5
2 LOVE BEFORE HURT	25
3 LOVE AFTER HURT	63
4 BLOOD IS THICKER THAN WATER. SO?	95
5 WHO THE SON SETS FREE IS FREE INDEED	113
6 EVERYBODY HAS THEM	125
7 WELL, MAMA'NEM DID IT LIKE THIS	141
8 HERE'S WHERE I DRAW THE LINE	163
9 FIND YOUR TRIBE	187
10 WHO DAT WOMAN? (OR MAN)	197
11 EH? SO YOU THOUGHT?	213
12 HEY, ME! GET OUT OF MY OWN WAY!	219
ACKNOWLEDGEMENTS	242

Introduction

Hey Friend! I am so glad that you are here.

There could be any reason that you decided to pick up this book and spend some time with me. Whatever the reason, I am glad you decided to, and I hope you find something relatable once you dive in.

As I was writing this book, I thought about who I was in different stages of my life verses who I have become. All that thinking took me back down memory lane.

I often reminisce on my childhood years when I hear the catchy hook lyrics of the popular nineties' song, Back in the Day, blaring from my car's radio. If this West Coast hip-hop classic is just as unforgettable to you as it is to me, you may be able to relate to the sentiments of the song. Back in the Day is a staple song for a staple generation growing up during that time. But really, do you wish you were a kid again? Asking a group of people that question will get a variety of answers.

As for me, Nah. I'm good.

I don't say that because I was abused or neglected in my early childhood. Adulting does come with many responsibilities, but I like the ability to be able to think for myself and

INTRODUCTION

make my own choices—something childhood didn't offer much of.

I didn't have a hard childhood. I mean, I was a little traumatized by those irritating white tights, itchy lace on those little cute dresses and the no-bang hairstyles which made my big forehead stand out that my mom insisted on punishing me with. I preferred the line in the bangs from the pink sponge rollers that set overnight to no bang any day. Yes, in my very young mind, those felt like punishments to say the least.

At home, I had it easy from what I could see. I came from a structured, Christ-centered home. I wouldn't say that I was sheltered, but I was parented well. I learned right from wrong, what was good and bad and how to be what is considered "well-mannered." My mom was the disciplinary, but my dad did not come short of giving instruction when he saw it to be necessary. His instruction came as small as correcting me and my siblings for putting our elbows on the dinner table while we were eating to as important as teaching us the bible.

Since my dad is a pastor, I was raised in the church. There were several days that I sat in our den and listened to read-a-long bible books that echoed stories in animated voices about Joseph and his colorful coat to Naaman and his initial refusal to dip seven times in the Jordan River.

Between all the many hours over the course of years I spent in church and the obligatory at-home bible studies, I did not fall short of knowing God's Word. Despite all our church going, many people think that preacher's kids are nothing close to innocent. In fact, the comical rumor I hear in the streets about us PKs is that we are the worst kids out of everyone's kids. Though I consider myself a person of integrity and of great character, I most certainly do carry plenty of flaws. I wouldn't say that I was any worse than the average kid though.

I have most definitely made just as many mistakes as the average person. Having the upbringing that I had does not make me exempt from shortcomings.

My role as a therapist often reminds me of the magnifying glass that burns over you as a PK. Because I am a therapist, my human reactions or behaviors can be harshly judged. Therapist is my occupation. I come bearing my experiences as me, April. Not a therapist. Just me. The conversations of this book are some that I have pondered sharing for quite some time. I've been itching to prove to myself that I am so unashamed that I can be this transparent to the world about my imperfections, the things that held me back, and the things that set me free.

While my book is far from a tell-all as my husband jokingly calls it, it surely tests my comfort level about sharing my mistakes and the poor choices that created some of these experiences. The hardest part about writing the stories was including others because it's human nature to not want to hear the way someone experienced you as anything short of peaches, cream, and red roses.

However, the reality is, other people are largely a part of our stories. Even if they don't like our perception of how we might have been affected by their actions, we still have to be brave enough to share our story of healing and growth.

The stories in this book are a compilation of experiences that shaped me in many ways from early childhood to teenage life, early adulthood, and onward.

We need freedom from things, and we need freedom to do things. Since I am the protagonist of my life, and there are so many different layers of life in general, it took a lot of self-awareness and self-examination to come to realize the ways in which I needed to be set free and what I needed freedom from, what I needed to be free to do, and who I needed to be free to be.

With all that I have learned and all that there is left to learn, I can honestly say that I have been set free from so much, and I feel blessed to walk in those freedoms.

INTRODUCTION

I hope that as you enjoy learning about some of the ways that I accomplished those freedoms that you can find ways in which you can relate and ways that you can be free.

One
YOU CAN RUN BUT CAN YOU HIDE?

"People think of the word *fearless* to mean without fear. I see it to actually mean 'with fear but you do it anyway'."
—Luvvie Ajayi Jones

As a small child, I was fearless when it came to certain things. I would climb trees without a second thought of what could happen if I fell. I wasn't thinking about breaking my arms, legs—or worse—my neck as I climbed up the huge oak tree on the side of my northside childhood home in Jacksonville, Florida.

Being the youngest of six children, I sometimes thought I had to prove that I was smart enough and strong enough to do things that they thought I couldn't or wouldn't do.

I was the "fearless" one out of myself and my brother Tony who decided to allow my brothers Chris and Rob to launch me off a ghetto homemade see-saw built in our very own yard, made with wood, bricks, and springs, which landed me in the emergency room. The seesaw incident was the joint effort between Chris and Rob.

Looking back, I really believe they set out to get rid of baby sis once and for all that day. What better way to do it than to launch me off that seesaw? I'm sure that Chris is happy that they didn't take me out because he and I have become the best of friends.

Since Tony and I were only one year apart in age, I was often in competition with him. Tony refused to stand on one end of the seesaw while one of them jumped on the other, so I decided I would be the stunt dummy—literally.

I took my wrongful place at the end of the seesaw. As soon as Robert with all his solid teenage weight landed on the other end, all fifty-five pounds—if that—of my petite eight-year-old body flew up in the air, through the tree branches, and landed on the ground with my head to a red brick.

My slow reaction to the shock is still the funniest part of the story to me. I giggled as I began to raise my body slowly up off the ground—until I saw the blood on the brick. Then I realized blood was running down my face. *There was so much blood!*

Now, it wasn't funny anymore, and I was scared more than hurt. I jumped up, and I ran toward the front of the house hollering, and Tony was right behind me bawling his eyes out too. My mom must have heard me hollering because she met us in the foyer as we entered the house. Here stood her little frail and fragile baby girl standing in front of her bleeding from a big fresh gash in her forehead. Whatever emotions she felt when she saw me didn't deter her from springing into action.

Tony held me in a hug, and we both cried loudly as I bled onto his blue jersey. In that moment, I realized that Tony had made the smarter choice when he refused to let Chris and Rob talk him into getting on that seesaw.

My mom quickly came back carrying her purse and a rag for my forehead. We left for the hospital.

Once in the emergency room, I was examined immediately. The doctor told my mom he had to stitch up the deep gash. Hearing this, I cried dramatically. *The doctor was going to stick a needle in my head!*

My mother, probably full of anxiety herself, and my anxiety not making it any better, threatened to leave me alone with the doctor while he stitched me up if I didn't "hush all that hollering." I stifled the cries. The last thing I wanted was to be left alone with the doctor who was sewing up my head. I left the hospital with stitches, a white bandage across the top right side of my forehead, and a new fear.

The "seesaw makers" got a good ole-fashioned butt whooping when we got back from the hospital. I remember feeling sorry about them getting in big trouble.

Though I acted out of fearlessness, it also was not the smartest thing to be fearless about. That was one of the things in my childhood that taught me to fear doing things that I think might cause me to get hurt—or even worse, to die.

As I got older, I still desired to do adventurous things but would run multiple anxious reasons through my head about why I should not do most of the adventurous ventures Boss has challenged me to during our marriage. Though fearful, nothing he's gotten me to do with him has taken much convincing. How can I resist making such unforgettable memories with the love of my life, right?

Honestly, every single frightening thing I've done with Boss I have not regretted making those memories. Don't get me wrong, I was scared—very scared—but I still followed through with all his ideas.

I would be lying if I said he is the only one that comes up with some of the things we do. I have also come up with bright ideas to do the things I am afraid to do too. I do them scared because I want to create those memories with my husband and to gain the experiences for myself. The water sports challenged my fears the most.

Living near Destin, Florida, we were surrounded by beautiful beaches with emerald green water and white sand. I never liked going to the beach much until we moved to Destin. Our hometown beaches are not comparable to the beaches sitting on the Gulf of Mexico in Florida's Panhandle.

After we got married, we moved to a small town-like city called Crestview. A twenty-minute traffic-free drive down 85 would easily take us to Fort Walton Beach. About fifteen more minutes of passing through Okaloosa Island down the coast of 98, and we'd be in Destin. The Beaches in that area stretched miles long.

When goggling *Things to Do in Destin,* a myriad of water activity results will surface—water activities that I am afraid to do, like parasailing, for one. So here we were living in this tourist town where most of everything fun to do had to do with water.

For our third Anniversary, Boss surprised me with a parasailing excursion. I was eight weeks postpartum. My sister-in-law Erika and my brother Rob came into town to visit. Boss used their visit as a perfect babysitting opportunity. We headed to the beach with our four children and their three children in tow. We picked a spot on the beach for Rob, Erika and the kids to spread out, near where our boat would be leaving.

We were not the only duo on the boat, but I believe we were the first to go up. As we were being strapped into the safety harness preparing to go up in the air, I was terrified. You hear me? Ter-ri-fied! I had just had a new baby, and God knows I wanted to live to see him grow up. My mind was going crazy with fearful thoughts, but I was not about to chicken out. I was not about to tell my husband that I no longer had the guts to do one of the things on the top of our to-do list that I agreed I wanted to do also.

I triple checked the tightness of my harness, which was strapped over my shoulders and between my legs. I was praying as our parachute was lifted steadily from the boat with my life attached to it. Before I knew it, Boss and I were side by side floating in the air with the boat moving forward below us.

It was so peaceful up there. So quiet. I felt free and liberated. In that moment, nothing else mattered.

Honestly, I felt closer to God. Could have been because I had just prayed going up there or because this was a near-death experience. I'm partially joking about the near-death experience.

I don't know if I've ever felt that at peace before. It was a feeling of leaving everything behind and just being in the moment. Nothing was in our reach that could have taken that moment away. No ringing phones, no notification sounds. We couldn't hear much of anything. We couldn't escape the moment ourselves by reaching for anything other than each other.

Today, I would identify that as a mindful experience. I was no longer afraid; I just felt peaceful. There was no place else at that moment I would have rather been but up in the air with my best friend, creating a memory I hope to never forget.

Despite my fears, the parasailing turned out to be a much more peaceful, calming experience than the next excursion I trusted good-old trustworthy Boss Jones to lead the way on—the Jet Skis.

YOU CAN RUN BUT YOU CAN'T HIDE

Jet-skiing out to one of Destin's hot spots, Crab Island, was on our list, so I was going to do that too. Fearful or not. Dressed in our swimsuits, we arrived at the Harbor Walk Village. The boardwalk is about a quarter mile stretch of restaurants, shops and water sport rentals. We rented one Jet Ski to ride together—I was too afraid to drive on my own.

Pulling off from the boardwalk on the two-person Jet Ski with the Crab Island sandbar in our view, we set out for our destination. It was less than a half a mile away. We followed the sign's instructions and idled our way through the non-wake zones along with the other water vessels that were going and coming.

Once we were in the clear to ride the waves freely, we zipped around Crab Island, enjoying the breeze. I held on tightly with my arms snuggled around my man's waist and relaxed into his body. *Ahhh, this is the life,* I thought.

The scenery was beautiful as usual. Crab Island was like an outside venue for a big boat party during the summer months. We kept our distance from the anchored boats that were clustered together and securely settled on top of the shallow parts of the water. Some parts of the water surrounding the boats were shallow enough to stand with your head above the clear water. The tourists and residents swam, socialized, and laid out on their boat decks enjoying the calm waters and balmy weather. Children enjoyed the huge bounce house that floated atop the water, securely anchored.

We rode out farther past the huddled boats where the water was no longer clear and beautiful but dark and murky. Some areas were shallow, some deep. My fear of being out there lingered in the back of my mind, but I was enjoying every bit of my ride.

Boss was steadily driving and keeping the ride as smooth as possible against the waves. Suddenly, he must have had a change of heart because he maneuvered a donut, and in a split second, everything changed.

The moment I felt myself plunging into the lukewarm water, I was calling on Jesus. I can swim but trying to swim was ironically the last thing on my mind. I was flailing around in the water until I heard Boss' voice: "Just stand up."

When I opened my eyes, he was standing next to me, laughing. The water stopped around his mid stomach. When I realized I could stand up in the water and I was not drowning—with my life vest on—all I could do was laugh hysterically.

Now ain't this a beach! There we were, standing out in a shallow part of the ocean, far from any parts of the shore, laughing so hard we could barely hoist ourselves back up on the Jet Ski. I had the most trouble getting back up there.

To this day, Boss claims we were not in the middle of the ocean. I disagree. We were in the middle of the ocean because where was the land? I surely couldn't see it.

Although I was so glad when our hour time limit was up on that Jet Ski, I had no regrets. It was scary, and it was fun. I am not saying I won't fearfully do it again, but I haven't been back on a Jet Ski since then. That was eleven years ago.

Those are some of the types of things a person can fear but can convince themselves to do more of or never again. Once they are over, we are no longer experiencing the feeling of fear anymore. In fact, I felt a sense of thrill during the ride. After the ride was over, I felt a sense of relief and happiness at the same time. I was relieved that we came out unscathed and joyful because I enjoyed it. Those are the types of things I can be afraid of but do it anyway, which is a good thing when it comes to making memories.

I faced my fear of flying for the first time when I flew on a non-stop flight to Virginia with six of my family members.

YOU CAN RUN BUT YOU CAN'T HIDE

I am afraid of flying, I had to face my fears if I wanted to be present on that trip. If I allowed fear to keep me off airplanes, I would not have visited as many places nor created some of the memories I have with friends and family.

Every time I fly, I face that fear. Sure, I would love to be able to jump on flights without experiencing fear and anxiety. Since that isn't my reality, I do the best I can. Each time, I prepare myself for what I know is coming.

The anxiety begins when I am booking the flight, then it settles after I've booked it. Sometimes I procrastinate a little when booking flights. I might choose the flight and not book it until days later. I might come up with excuses in my head as to why the trip can wait, then talk myself back into it. The anxiety resurfaces closer to the flight date, and man, oh, man, during the flight, if I don't prepare for other things to focus on, the anxiety will be on ten and I will be keyed up inside and praying for the entire flight!

I manage the fear by choosing the airlines I am comfortable flying with. I book flights during the times of day I am most comfortable with flying, and if I can help it, I try not to fly alone. I am not calm enough to sleep on flights, and I can barely concentrate enough to read, so I download shows and movies to distract me the entire time.

If I am flying with my husband, and the plane is jolted with turbulence, I hold his hand. I do the best I can to not allow fear to stop me from experiencing the things in life I would like to experience—like seeing places and visiting people. When I get off that flight, I enjoy my trip while creating new memories, and I am grateful that I did it.

Unfortunately, all the things feared are not that simple to be over and done with. Some of my fears are easier to manage than others. The greatest, longest fear I have ever had is of dogs. Although I had a fear of doing the things I mentioned earlier, I do not have triggers associated with them in the same manner as I do with my fear of dogs, which began early in my childhood.

One of my favorite aunts lived across the street from my childhood home. Her house sat diagonally across to the left of our Grand Park home. Both homes occupied lots on two of the four corners of 15th and Canal Street.

Not many days after the seesaw incident—my head still bandaged over the stitches I had gotten—I was at my aunt's house preparing to leave for a wedding rehearsal for a dear friend of hers who had chosen me to be a flower girl.

Her neighbor had two large tan pit bulls tied up on the side of her house. As my aunt and I walked out of her back door and up the side of the house toward the driveway, her neighbor's pit bull barked. One of them broke its chain.

As he charged toward us, we ran around the house to the front yard. As we both ran to save our lives, we split up. My Aunt found a hiding place behind a big bush near the front door of her house. I jetted, with my heart racing faster than a Camaro locked in first place at the Daytona 500, running as fast as my little legs could carry me toward Canal Street. I gave no thought to exercise the street crossing rules I had been taught. Before I ran into the busy traffic, the pit pounced on me, bringing me to the ground. I could hear my aunt screaming frantically for my uncle's help.

"Dennnniiis! Dennnniiis!"

Mr. D must not have been too far behind us because just as quickly as the dog had pounced on me, he was pulling him off me even quicker. Everything happened so fast. I was shaken to my core. I trembled and cried.

I already was not fond of animals, but since that day, I have been terrified of dogs. Tiny dogs, small dogs, big dogs, you name it. On days when I had to walk home alone from the bus stop, I was terrified. I was afraid that I would encounter a loose dog. Some days I did.

There was this one red brick house near my elementary school bus stop, where a little brown Chihuahua lived. The dog had dug a hole right under the galvanized steel fence with just enough room for it to squeeze its tiny body out and chase me whenever it saw me walk by. Chihuahua might be one of the smallest breeds of dogs, but they are the biggest bullies.

One day in particular, the Chihuahua came running and yapping, I dropped my book bag and anything else I might have been carrying, and I took off down the street toward home.

I saw the seesaw makers—Chris and Rob—walking up the street toward me, apparently arriving late to meet me at the bus stop. I was relieved when I saw them because they could go back for my book bag—so I thought.

They both stood there and watched as they made me go back in front of that dog's house to collect my own things. As I picked up my belongings as quickly but quietly as I could, I was grateful the Chihuahua had gone back into its fence and no longer seemed interested in me.

Perhaps my brothers thought it was ridiculous that I was so afraid of such a small dog. They might have thought making me go back to get my book bag on my own was showing me that there was nothing to be afraid of. It didn't work. The fear and anxiety I felt was real and intense. To this day, I am still afraid to walk alone in any neighborhood out of fear that I might encounter a dog.

That fear is reinforced every time I see someone post a picture and a message in our neighborhood social media group to alert our neighbors that their dog has gotten out and is wandering around.

On the day that the pit bull broke its chain, it did not bite me. However, the sound of the chain breaking has stuck with me since. So much so that, even now, if I hear a similar sound, my nervous system responds, and my heart begins to race. It can be the sound of keys dropping or rattling or an actual sound of a chain. Those sounds trigger an immediate trauma response.

Several of my colleagues have suggested exposure therapy. I've respectfully declined each time. However, the fear of small dogs has gotten better with time and with some unplanned exposure outside of therapy.

It would be several years later and not many years ago, that I would have my second and even scarier encounter with a pit bull. This time my friend's dog. I spotted the dog in my peripheral vision as I sat in her living room settled between a high bar table and a bar chair that sat against a wall.

He had wondered outside of the designated room he was supposed to be sheltered in during my visit. Unlike my earlier encounter with my aunt's neighbor's pit bull, this time, I was blocked in. I had nowhere to run so my body could not respond in its normal flight defense.

Briefly, the entire room went black. For seconds, I had no idea what was going on around me. It was like my brain was telling my body to shut down to escape the danger I was in. I was not consciously in the room when the dog approached me. It was not until I mentally reentered the room that I noticed my hand was wet from the dog's lick.

After I got my friend's daughter's attention with a yell, she quickly came.

"What are you doing in here?" she asked as she grabbed his collar.

"Y'all left the door opened," I told her.

She took the dog back to where he escaped from and secured the doors shut.

My legs were jelly. I could barely stand, and for about ten minutes, I was shaky. That is the true meaning of "I was shook."

Since this fear began with a traumatic event that happened in my early childhood many years ago, some might think that I should be over it by now. I've been judged at different times and even noticed others' frustration when my fear has shown up during different situations.

I can admit that my intense fear of dogs can be an inconvenience to those around me at times. Many dog owners love to assert how sweet and harmless their dog is when they learn of my discomfort. My body does not care how highly people speak of their dogs. Unfortunately, preaching to me how sweet their dog is and praising their accolades does not settle the fear nor does it increase any amount of trust that I have in any dog. I wish it were that simple.

Knowing that not everyone will understand nor empathize, I have learned not to judge myself for how my body responds to the fear that this early childhood experience evoked in me. I have been careful to acknowledge what little progress I've made over the years. Honestly, I have never had a goal to completely rid the fear of dogs. I know that I can run from this fear, but I can't hide from it.

As I have gotten older, I learned to manage it the best I can when I am confronted with it. I just know that sometimes I must operate through that fear. Fear makes us want to avoid things. Honestly, sometimes I do avoid doing the things that will bring the discomfort of that fear, but I will compromise with myself.

I avoid walking alone in neighborhoods, but I will walk with a companion, anxious or not. I prefer not to visit people's houses with dogs, but sometimes I choose to visit despite the fear—if they put their dogs away. I will allow myself into uncomfortable situations sometimes, despite the fear, if I see it as beneficial.

My mother-in-law has a dog named Cookie. To accompany Boss to her house, I must work through the presence of that fear while I am there. I will not pet Cookie, nor will I sit in the same room with her. I am anxious and mostly uncomfortable the entire time, but I go. That is my efforts to operate through fear.

Oddly enough and contrary to everything I just shared about my fear of dogs, I suggested we get a puppy. I wanted a small, cute puppy. I convinced Boss to purchase a white fluffy Bichon Frisé from a local pet store.

Graci was nine weeks old when we got her. She was small enough to sit in my hands and would grow to weigh no more than eighteen pounds and twelve inches in height.

As we traveled from the pet store to our home, Graci sat on a cardboard box top on my lap trembling and looking at me look back at her with the same small ounce or two of anxiety she was feeling.

It took a few days for me to get used to her. Opening myself up to becoming a dog owner despite my intense fear of dogs was a huge step for me. We had two boys, nine and thirteen years old, and an eleven-year-old daughter when we brought Graci into our lives. The kids fell in love with her immediately.

Unfortunately, during my third and last pregnancy, I was too sick to care for Graci. She was just nine months old when we rehomed her to a family member.

When I decided to bring Graci home, I did something I wanted to do without allowing fear and anxiety to stop me. While growing through my fears, I realized that it is okay to give myself credit for the efforts I make, big or small. It is okay to push myself beyond that fear. Looking at fear in a broader way, if we allow it to run our lives, most of us will not live life outside of those fears.

Like me, you may have some long-standing fears that are triggered by things that happened in your childhood as well or at any time in your life. As you read this, you might be recalling some things that you love doing or would like to do but have not allowed yourself to enjoy because of the discomfort of fear and anxiety. It seems easier to run from fear, but then so much may go undone.

It has brought me joy when I try my best to do the things that I really want to do anyway—when I do all the things through the anxiety, when I do them even in the presence of fear. I've tried not to allow fear to stop me from pursuing my dreams, from creating memories, and being present where I would like to show up.

I was stepping out on faith while filled with anxiety when I made the transition from a full-time job with the state making guaranteed money to a contractor with a mental health agency with no idea if I would be able to keep enough clients for half of a case load—much less a full case load.

However, if I wanted to reach my goal of becoming a licensed mental health provider, I had to manage through my fear. There was no hiding from them. The opportunity that was presented to me caused me to have to confront several fears. The fear of going into people's homes—many of which had dogs. The fear of what my case load would look like, how that would affect us financially, and one of the most common fears when beginning a new career—if I was good enough. If I had what it took to be able to help people with their mental health while maintaining ethical obedience to *do no harm*.

My exit interview was scheduled with the director who was a Caucasian woman appearing to be several years my senior. As I sat across from her, I was cheesing my behind off. Gushing with joy. I could not stop grinning from ear-to-ear. I tried so hard to swipe the grin off my face. I giggle just thinking about it. I was sitting there the whole time thinking about how I was not only beginning an internship for my dream career, but I was also getting paid during this internship with the potential to make great money.

When you're great at what you do, no company wants to lose you. They weren't too fond of my leaving. I had been asked by the center manager to stay part-time. I turned down the offer.

During the exit interview, the director said something that could have easily cast doubt in my spirit, but I was in too high a place to accept any negativity or allow it to bring me down. Mentally, I felt great.

"You do know being a mental health therapist is stressful?" she asked rhetorically, as if to insinuate that I can't handle it. This was her way of reminding me about the times I was overwhelmed in this current position. However, some of the way the program was run was the most stressful, not the actual job responsibilities.

I just kept right on grinning. I wanted to get that exit interview over with as quickly as possible so I could be on my way. Although I did have my own doubts and fears about the uncertainty and the unknown, I was proud of myself. Nothing was going to steal my joy. Not even the grimace on her face or her attempt to dissuade me with her half comment, half question. I walked out of there with a juxtaposition of emotions, both excited, ready for the challenge of my new career and full of anxiety, all at the same time.

It's astonishing how the body reacts to protect itself when the fear emotion is triggered. Dogs are not the only thing that I've run away from.

When my dad got sick in the pulpit many years ago, the traumatic event left me with post-traumatic stress disorder. Several years had gone by before I realized that I had developed PTSD. It was not until after I studied mental disorders and talked to a therapist, that it dawned on me.

My dad was on the program to preach on this night during a weeklong assembly that he held annually at his church.

YOU CAN RUN BUT YOU CAN'T HIDE

The church was packed with current members, former members and visitors. After the master of ceremony had introduced him, he took his place at the podium.

Not long after he began his message he turned and addressed one of the preachers who sat behind him. "Take over, brother I'm sick." He set the mic on the podium and walked off the pulpit, exiting through the door that led into his pastoral office.

It took a few seconds for it to register with me what was going on. After my mom got up and headed to the back of the church, I followed—along with several others—to check on him.

Immediately after reaching the door of the hallway leading to the bathrooms and his office, the first person I saw was my mother. She stood facing the corner of the wall, her back turned to the door, frantically crying to God, "Lord please don't let me see my husband like this," she prayed.

When I realized that my father was lying on the floor just outside of the men's restroom, barely conscious, I did a 180 and ran across the back of the sanctuary and toward the door.

I ran out of the church doors into the dark, cool October night and just kept going. I don't know where I was going, but my mind said go, and my body reacted.

Before I could make it out of the church's yard, my pregnant bestie, Kisa, stopped me. She tackled me to the ground like a defensive back. She was right behind me when I ran out of the door, but I didn't notice. After seeing my dad on the floor, I was totally oblivious to everyone around.

She and her mom—my Auntea Debbie—were successful in calming me down by reassuring me that everything was going to be okay.

The service was not yet over but was being closed out with prayer for my dad by my uncle. Some of the congregates had migrated outside.

My dad is like a father to many people. I can remember one of the younger preachers standing outside hitting the brick building with the side of his fist and praying passionately.

There was certainly a lot going on outside. The ambulance had arrived, but I had no idea what was going on inside. The EMTs entered the church before my older sister, Carol, came out of the door. Carol was known to be one of all my siblings who handles everything calmly and logically in my eyes. I could see that she was crying and one of Dad's sisters exited behind her doing the same except she was bawling hysterically. Seeing their reactions to whatever was happening inside set me off again. I instantly assumed the worst.

"What happened?!" I screamed to no one in particular.

Right before I went back into full panic mode, Auntea Debbie gently placed her hand on my arm.

"Look," she said, pointing toward the ambulance. "He's okay. They are taking him to the hospital."

The EMTs had exited the side door of the church. My dad lay on the stretcher with an oxygen mask over his mouth and nose as they pushed him onto the ambulance.

For a long time after that night, it took every amount of will and power inside of me to step inside of that church. I was afraid to go watch him preach. Every time there was a pause in his message, it was a trigger for me.

The night he got sick while he was preaching, he paused and fumbled the mic a little, and so every time I was sitting on the pew, and he paused I felt stuck. I froze like a deer's gaze in a headlight. The fear emotion struck me at each pause. If I happened to be looking down at the time of his pause, I wouldn't look up until I heard his next words as if looking up too soon would cause a replay, and the entire real-life nightmare would happen all over again.

YOU CAN RUN BUT YOU CAN'T HIDE

It took me a while to be comfortable going into the back of the church near the bathrooms where he lay in his own blood that night.

On a lot of Sundays, I just didn't go to church. When I did go, I was uneasy and anxious the entire service, and could not concentrate. I was antsy, counting the minutes until church was over so I could get out of there and get some peace of mind. Eventually, I would visit another church, and my absences would start to increase at my dad's church.

I begin to think about death a lot, and the frequent thoughts created an unhealthy fear of those close to me dying. I often had nightmares of my father dying, and I also daydreamed, replaying the night he got sick in my mind over and over at random times. Carol is the go-to person my parents call in the time of trouble. I dreaded answering the phone anytime she called, fearful that she would be calling to tell me what I feared the most.

Some fears can be overbearing and crippling. Those are the fears we may need to seek help for. I tried to deal with the fear on my own, thinking time will help. It did help somewhat, but not to the extent that I needed it to. God put knowledgeable people in place to help us through hard things. I had to work this fear out with prayer and in therapy. I am still not one hundred percent unphased by that night, but I have come a long way.

Kisa asked me, "What I wanna know is, where were you going to run to that night?"

I laughed. "I don't know." All I know is my body did the first thing that my brain told it to do: Run.

Some of my struggles with fear are due to trauma. It does not matter how big or small it may seem; I am careful to be self-compassionate. These are things I am experiencing, but they are not a character flaw or weakness. Our body and brain work together in interesting ways during a trauma response. It helps to learn our triggers and seek understanding regarding how the traumatic event may be influencing our thoughts and feelings—contributing to the fear.

Years later, I wrote a poem titled "My Greatest Fear." I read it to my first therapist years ago. It was a tremendous help with processing that trauma.

I've heard many people say they do not share their fear for the fear of someone using it against them. Some people carry the belief that admitting fear is a sign of weakness. This alone shows how much of a stronghold fear can have over a person's thinking. I've worked through my fears enough to be comfortable sharing them.

Fear is a type of emotion that you can run from, but it's going to be pretty darn hard to hide from. The good thing is that it is manageable. It might not be an easy emotion to manage, especially when the fear is tied to trauma—but it is manageable, nonetheless.

Through my experiences with my own fears and anxiety, I have learned that I could carry both courage and fear simultaneously. Despite the fears that consume me at times, I know I am brave in many ways. As I have grown, so has my courage. One of the great things I have discovered about courage is that courage is not the absence of fears, but it is the ability to face the fears and grow despite its presence.

YOU CAN RUN BUT YOU CAN'T HIDE

My Greatest Fear by April Brown

Ever since the night that it happened something ain been right with me.
I've been bound with ridiculous sounds that won't let me be free.
Ever since it happened six years ago seems like yesterday.
When everyone in the building except me could do was just pray.
I couldn't pray, I couldn't get a word out to God that night.
I just completely fell apart.
Like a coward, I ran for the door but didn't know where my fear would lead me.
I just wanted to run, run and run some more.
I ran from the fear of losing someone I have loved from the day I was born, and ever since that night I have been completely torn.
I say all the time to myself, Girl, you couldn't even stay and pray, but my God, I am sorry but how could I stand there and see my daddy that way.
In a state I had never seen him before,
weak, laying almost breathless in his own blood,
while everyone prayed over him pleading for God's healing power.
Who knew when I ran out that door that night, I would be running into another door of a never-ending fight.
Till this day the reoccurring dreams keep playing out with the same scenes of him being snatched away and me running instead of staying to pray.
Even wide awake, my idle mind sets itself on neutral and those dreams become daydreams.
I find myself awake dreaming, of me running, crying and screaming.
I think my goodness, it's been six years, and I am still living day by day with the same fears.
Why does that night keep coming back to me?
Why can't those memories just let me be free?
Why do I still want to say,
"daddy sit down, you've preached enough" right in the middle of a message?
I think that is some crazy stuff.
I keep going back to a church where I want to be but then again where I don't want to be.
I keep thinking,
I would rather be absent if it happens again
because I'm afraid of reliving the night that all this begin.
This is my greatest fear!

Two
LOVE BEFORE HURT

"I will not try to convince you to love me, to respect me, to commit to me. I deserve better than that. I am better than that. Goodbye."
—Unknown

Falling in love is a risky business. We are opening ourselves up to the possibility of being hurt by someone we love. I don't believe love hurts. It is the acts that are done outside of what love is that hurt. Can someone love you and hurt you? Of course. The fact that they love you doesn't make the hurtful actions any less significant or less painful.

Some people are stuck in survival mode, and they operate from that place. Some are carrying trauma-filled baggage, and the open wounds that come with that weight, so they bleed onto you. The emotion of loving someone is one thing, but the action takes work. Love is both a feeling and an action word.

LOVE BEFORE HURT

I believe my ex-husband loved me by the way he felt about me. Some of his actions were out of love in his own way, but he was not capable of showing me the love I deserved. I loved him before the hurt. I loved him through the hurt, then I decided the hurt was too much a burden to bear in the name of love.

When I met him, I was less than a month shy of 17 years old and in my junior year of high school. I met him through a friend named Tiffany who was from out of state. She came to Florida to live with her older sister. We met through our sisters. My oldest sister and her older sister were best friends.

Tiffany and I instantly clicked from the day we met. We would hang out on some weekends at either of our sister's houses listening to music, taking walks, just typical teenage stuff. That is, until that not so typical joy ride that I will spill the beans about later.

Her thick Milwaukee accent combined with her outspokenness added humor to her candor personality. I liked her style. Her go-to hair style was a fan ponytail. She wore it neatly brushed together and gelled down with her edges laid for the gods.

We stood outside of her sister's apartment in the parking lot when she introduced me to Kelvin. He was tall and slim with a deep dark brown skin complexion and a nicely combed out afro. I stood shyly as he smiled at me showing off his dimples. Back then, I saw a cute swag that I attributed to his long bowlegs. The old white box Cadillac he drove matched his swag. It's funny how an attraction can go from one hundred to zero after coming to terms with who a person really is.

He introduced himself to me as Kevin, no *L*. Although not far from it, I thought that Kevin was his real name for quite some time. When I heard from a mutual party that the correct way to pronounce his name was with an L, I looked at his driver's license, and indeed it reflected his legal name as Kelvin. I continued to call him Kevin. So did a lot of other people, including Tiffany and his best friend who she was dating at the time. Maybe he liked Kevin better so that's what he wanted people to call him. I still dismiss the L today.

For a while, Tiffany accompanied us when we hung out. Hanging out with an older guy was a little awkward for me, at first. I had never hung out with a guy so many years older than me. All my guy friends and any boyfriends that I had were in high school, like me. Not only did his age set him apart from the majority of the guys I interacted with on a day-to-day basis, but he was also a hustler.

Kelvin's "occupation" was not something I could go home and brag to mama and daddy about. Here I was, the seventeen-year-old PK out there in the streets of Jacksonville, dating a twenty-one-year-old man who was *out there in them streets*. If anyone thinks that I was young and dumb, I won't disagree. Trust me, I know I fit the description quite well then. There was a lot I didn't know, but like most teenagers, I thought I knew a lot more than I truly did.

Not only was I dating someone I knew my parents would not approve of, unbeknownst to me, he happened to be one of our church members' nephews and the cousin of one of my closest friends, Tip.

It was not long after we began dating and I had gotten a lot more comfortable with him that we realized we were super tight with the same person.

One day Kelvin and I were chatting on the phone as I lay in my bedroom. I mentioned something about my cousin Tiffany (Tip is what I call her in this book to separate the two Tiffany's).

"Tiffany? Wait a minute. Where does she live?" he asked.

"Off Kings Road," I answered, sitting up straight.

After I gave him her last name, he told me she is his cousin.

"She isn't my real cousin. We just call each other cousins," I quickly clarified.

The worst part about finding out that he was related to Tip is that I knew as soon as her mom found out that we were dating, she was going to snitch. And she did. Not that she cared one bit about how I felt, but I was furious with her. As a teenager I thought, *Why couldn't she just mind her business?!*

At the time, she would come over to the house to help my mom with her in-home daycare. When she was there, I made sure to play on repeat R. Kelly's "The Sermon" right at the part where he preaches about folks minding their business. That song hit differently in that moment.

As a teenager with a "you don't know him like I do" attitude, I didn't understand the problem. Never mind, she had known him all his life, and I was still getting to know the parts of him he would allow me to see.

As an adult and parent looking back on the situation, I understand completely why she didn't mind her business, as the song said. She let my parents know that their seventeen-year-old daughter was dating a twenty-one-year-old man who she knew as someone who dated a lot of women and was in the streets doing everything but the Lord's work. Legally, in the state of Florida, we weren't breaking any laws, but this was about much more than age.

Upon finding out that I was talking to Kelvin and the type of person his aunt described him to be, my mom immediately forbad me to see him. I went into my bedroom, slammed the door, threw myself on the bed and cried.

Seconds later, my door swung open.

"You want me to tan your hide?!" My dad's voice boomed.

My dad, with his five-feet-nine inches of height and slim statue, stood in the frame of my bedroom door. He never yelled at me but apparently, I had gone too far by slamming that door. First, let me say that my dad is from Georgia, and secondly, he was born in the early forties. Yes, he did say "tan your hide." Do not judge his choice of *fuss* words.

I think my crying because they wouldn't allow me to see Kelvin transitioned into me crying because my daddy yelled at me. I didn't even know that was possible until then. In fact, I never witnessed Apostle Lewis yelling at many people at all, especially, not his baby girl. He is one of the gentlest men I have ever known.

He must have lost his mind, I thought. I can bet that he was thinking the same thing about me.

I wasn't a perfect child, but up until I met Kelvin, I had never given my parents any real problems. They had every reason to be concerned.

Word traveled fast in my family. If there's any business to tell it was getting told. The next thing I knew, my sisters Angela and Carol were calling. My sisters are eleven and thirteen years older than me. They thought they were Mama Two and Mama Three. They told my mom that even if she tried to stop me from seeing him, I would find a way to do it anyway. They were right. That truth does not come without consequences though. Whoever first said a hard head makes a soft behind is a genius.

I knew the lifestyle Kelvin was living when I was dating him. Years ago, as I reflected and looked back, I realized how I could have ruined my life when I was a teenager just by association.

We were riding together in my mom's 1982 Toyota Corolla when he asked me to stop by his baby mother's grandma's house to see his only child, Kiaria, who was a smart, beautiful and sassy three-year-old little girl.

My sister had nicely styled my hair in single plaits. When I drove up and stopped the car in the street on the side of her grandmother's house, his baby mother approached me at the driver's side.

"Did Kevin get your hair done?" she barked.

"No, my sister did my hair."

"Oh, because I was about to say, I'll snatch that hair out your head. He can't even buy his baby no shoes."

The two of them began to argue across me until he got out of the car. They got into a tussle. I sat in the car wondering how I got in the middle of this hot ghetto mess.

This would not be the last time I would see them get into a physical altercation. After seeing those altercations, it never crossed my mind that he might hit me one day. He never did. However, the red flag alerts about how he handles conflict was flapping extremely hard. I did all but took heed to the warning signs.

It wasn't long before he jumped back into the car and told me to drive off because they called the police. We were just a few blocks over when red and blue lights glared, and a siren chirped at us as a warning to pull over. We pulled over. Another police car pulled up.

We sat and waited as two black police officers approached my car. A male and a female cop. I was nervous that we were being pulled over. Not for the same reason many people of color are cautious about today, since access to social media has made us aware and privy to how even routine traffic stops can become deadly for us. I was nervous because I knew the altercation between Kelvin and his baby's mother was the reason for the stop. I was thinking she had told the police he hit her.

The officers said they were told we had drugs in the car, and they needed to search the car. I was praying this man had not gotten into the car with me with drugs on him.

When they searched the car, they found a silver pocketknife with a brown handle in my glove compartment that I had placed there. They decided that the knife was too long in inches to legally carry around. The knife had dried orange juice on it from when I cut an orange several days ago. I am pretty sure they knew I was innocent in all of this, but Kelvin was the one they wanted. They were familiar with him and what he did on the streets of the neighborhood they often patrolled.

Kelvin's pugnacity is what got him arrested. He became irate because he thought the search was unwarranted. He kept yelling to the officers, "She don't have nothing to do with this" between F bombs and other profanities. He was taken to jail for resisting arrest without violence.

There were no drugs in the car.

Without searching or handcuffing me, the lady officer led me in the backseat of her police car and told me to get in. I was not from the streets or street smart. I was nothing close to a hood chick or any of those other terms people use to describe girls who was about this kind of life.

I complied with no question. Everything was happening so fast. I did not fully understand how the heck I ended up in the back of a police car. I didn't understand why Kelvin was being arrested. I was confused. All kinds of thoughts were spinning around in my head. *Was I being arrested?*

After the police officer drove off with me still in the back seat, she gave me a good talk. She told me that I needed to stay away from him and that he was not anyone I should be hanging around with. Then she told me she was not arresting me. She took me home instead. I was not yet relieved. I did not know if I wanted to arrive home in the back of a police car or if it was safer for me to be taken to juvenile.

When we pulled up at my house, my mom opened the door. I hugged my mom and I burst into tears. The officer spoke to my mom and filled her in on why she was bringing me home. My mom didn't fuss, she didn't lecture.

Surprisingly, she laughed. "That's what you get. Now stay from around there."

She decided that I had learned my lesson when the police lady decided to take me on a scared straight ride. Mama Two and Mama Three—my sisters—called and forbad me to go back around there to that neighborhood again, too. Other than being dropped off to pick up the Corolla that had been abandoned when the officer took me home, I didn't, but that was still my man. I wasn't going away that easily. *Tuh!* I was young, blind and in love!

I have never been a ride or die because I did not plan on dying for anybody, but that police ride obviously didn't scare me enough to cause me to walk away. His stay in jail was brief, then we were reunited.

The way Kelvin had my head in the clouds, you would think he was the first guy I fell in love with. He was not. It was J before Kelvin. J had Kelvin beat in the bad boy department. He spent a lot of time in the streets selling drugs and stealing cars.

I know studies say that daddy girls are attracted to men like their fathers, but I fell in the percentage that was totally opposite. Getting involved with these types of guys was my way of breaking free from the pressure of the "church girl" standard that people expected from preachers daughters.

Carol was who I confided in after I had given up my virginity to J. Although we had used protection, I thought something was wrong a week later when I had a stomachache.

Could I be pregnant? I thought.

I didn't know much about conception, so I panicked. My mother did not sit me down and go through the whole birds and the bees talk with me. Discussing anything pertaining to the *woo woo* other than having a period was not happening. The sex education in our house was short and sweet. "Save yourself for marriage, fornication is a sin."

I called Carol crying and dropped the dime on myself. After my coital confessions, she made an appointment and took me to Planned Parenthood where I was administered a pregnancy test and was given my first packet of birth control pills. I threw the pills in my top drawer up under some underwear to hide them from my mom and never took them. I did not need to. After only that one time with the guy who slid away with my virginity, it never happened again. We broke up shortly after he got into some legal trouble. I saw him once after he got out of jail.

Five years after we broke up, I sat in my living room watching the news. I was in awe and total shock when the news story about my familiar friend—the first boy I was head over heels for—came across the screen. J had gotten locked up again and was killed not long after being released from prison. Although, it had been many years since we had last spoken, my heart still hurt over the sad and unfortunate news of his death.

The problem with me not taking the birth control when I was not partaking in any intercourse was that I didn't start taking them whenever I did begin again—with Kelvin.

I would be lying if I said my pregnancy did not come without a warning. On a Sunday morning, months before I got pregnant, my dad called me into his office at the church.

"It's been hard for me to catch up with you lately." He spoke with a delicate tone.

I sat quietly.

"I had a dream that you rebelled, and you got pregnant."

I continued to sit quietly as he talked to me. Everything he said went in one ear and out of the other. I was in love, and there was nothing anyone could do to change that. *Whew!* Little did I know, Daddy knew best.

When I found out I was pregnant, I was deathly afraid to tell my parents. The first adult I confided in was Carol.

"When are you going to tell mama?" She asked several times over the course of about a week.

"I don't know."

"Do you want me to tell her."

I hesitated and thought about it. "Yeah"

After she told my mom, my mom insisted I tell my dad. That was not something I was even close to prepared to do. Not because I thought he would yell or scream at me, but because I knew he would be disappointed. A daddy's girl telling her father that she did something that she thinks he will be gravely disappointed about is one of the worse feelings. Not to mention something he had warned me about.

I never told him. I didn't have the guts to sit in his face and tell him that his dream had manifested. Eventually, my mom told him. It didn't take her long. We never talked about it. We walked around ignoring the elephant in the room as if my belly wasn't growing bigger over time.

The breakdown before the breakthrough came when I went up for prayer on a Sunday close to the end of my pregnancy. After my dad laid his hand across my forehead and prayed for me, we held each other in a tight hug. He was standing there as my shoulder to cry on as I released the shame I had been carrying.

My son was loved by my family even before he made his entrance into the world. My mom went to the grocery store every Monday. She bought whatever cereal I craved from week to week. When the doctor suggested I get my iron levels up to avoid having to have a blood transfusion during delivery, she cooked liver and cabbage for me weekly.

My friend, Jameelah, along with help from some of my other friends, hosted my baby shower at her aunt's house. Due to my mom's religious beliefs, she didn't attend my baby shower because I was pregnant out of wed lock.

Although my mom was not present at the baby shower, she was present in the delivery room, along with Kelvin and his aunt who told my mom we were dating. After thirteen hours of labor, I gave birth to a seven-pound, six-ounce baby boy with beautiful dark brown skin and a head full of shiny black hair. He not only took his father's face, but he is also named after him. We call him KB.

It wasn't long after the birth of our first-born son that Kelvin and I broke up. He was truly living up to the reputation his aunt had warned me about. He was getting around with the women and was far from faithful to me. Sometimes he showed up to provide for our child and sometimes he didn't.

My dad, obviously annoyed with the entire situation, spilled the beans when I asked him for some money to help buy pampers.

"What is Kelvin doing, other than running around in the street with different women?" With frustration wrinkled across his forehead, he pushed his hand into his pocket and pulled out a wad of money. He peeled back a few bills and handed them to me.

I took the money and quietly thanked him. *He saw him with other women.* I thought.

My dad worked all over the city. He has his own carpentry business. All day long he repairs and add-on to homes. He could be on any side of town on any given day. I didn't ask him to clarify that for me. I knew deep down that meant he saw him.

I broke up with him for a combination of reasons. After having our son, my perspective about a lot of things changed. I no longer wanted a man that was not working a legal and legitimate job. I didn't want the drama with the women. I certainly was the most turned off by his lack of support for our son.

A few months later, he began showing up more often to see our son. He was contributing a lot more to the things that he needed. He eventually approached the topic of us getting back together. I don't know what made him decide that he was ready to settle down with me. I was entertained by the idea. He was my son's father. If he wanted an opportunity to do the right thing, I was going to give it to him. I was huge on giving the benefit of the doubt to most people who wanted my forgiveness and a second chance to prove themselves. It took me a long time to realize that forgiving doesn't always mean you have to reconnect with the person that hurt you.

If Kelvin and I were going to be together he knew that he was going to need to make some changes. He got a job at a warehouse to prove to me that he was serious about making things work. It didn't take a long time for me to take him back after he secured the job. We restarted our relationship with a clean slate.

In the late spring of 1998—Kelvin and I got married at the courthouse, went grocery shopping at Save-a-Lot on a seventy-five dollar budget, packed up my bedroom on a U-Haul, and moved across town into our two-bedroom apartment on the southside of Jacksonville with KB in tow, all in the same day.

My mom sat on the porch and watched as we loaded up the U-Haul. Later, I asked my mom why she didn't try to stop me. "You were going to do what you wanted to do anyway. You had to learn." She was right. Despite several other adults in my life who told me not to marry him, I still skipped off to the courthouse and said, "I do." Even if somebody would have sent Whoopie Goldberg when she played in the movie *Ghost* as Oda Mae Brown to say, "April, you in danger girl," I wouldn't have listened.

I was nineteen-years-old and married with an eight-month-old. The first few years of our marriage were not horrible. We were the typical married couple. We went to work, came home and took care of our son. We shared most of the household responsibilities, including pooling our money together for bills and necessities.

I have lived with two men in my life. Each time I was lucky to have men who kept the toilet seat down and pitched in to maintain a clean house. Kelvin didn't cook much, but he cleaned the heck out of the bathroom and kitchen.

Kelvin and I slept together tightly in my twin bed that I had brought from my parents' house. For a little while we didn't have any furniture in the living room. I came home one day and there was an old used sofa sitting in our living room. Him and God only knows where he got that thing from. The sofa reeked of cigarette smoke. He covered the beige couch with a bed sheet as if that was going to mask the strong nicotine scent coming from the worn-out fabric. I can only imagine the amount of third-hand smoke we must have inhaled from that couch.

We didn't start off with much, but our bills were getting paid, and we were eating well. We were doing alright until he slipped and fell into a puddle of water at work and broke his knee in three places. He was still working at the warehouse, and I was working at Bank of America in an entry level data entry position.

He couldn't work for a while until his knee healed and he was released from the doctor. He was receiving workers' compensation. The compensation checks were coming in very slowly and very low. We all know that bills don't wait for the money to roll in. The rent was still due on the first.

I sat on the bed and cried when I had to spend my entire paycheck to pay the rent. Even though we were broke, I can say that God provided. He always has.

Other than the financial struggles we were facing, we didn't have much other drama—except for some minor baby mama drama.

Kiaria was five years old when we were a year into our marriage. While checking my voicemail on my Nokia cell phone one day, Kiaria's voice came from the other end of the phone. She spoke in a low, soft tone with a little gibberish that I didn't fully understand. As I continued listening, I was able to make out something about me being "ugly" and then louder and plainer, I made out, "Blacky Smacky!" With an emphasis on the *ky* in the word smacky.

I laughed and shook my head. I knew she didn't make that phone call on her own, nor did she come up with those words to say. I still joke with Kiaria about this every now and again.

Things were a little rocky between me and her mom in the beginning. After some time and maturity, we were able to interact in a way that was healthy and beneficial to our daughter.

Blended families can be tough. It was an adjustment for all of us. Getting there wasn't easy, but eventually, we began to get along well. I can't thank her enough for allowing me to be a huge part of her daughter's life.

Kelvin was always able to get good jobs when he applied himself. He had a great work ethic. He sought out warehouse work. He had no problem getting hired for the positions he applied for. In addition to his forklift position, he also worked with a good friend of his transporting corpses.

I rode with him on a few jobs to pick up bodies. The first time I rode with him, it was about an hour drive to a nearby city. The van we rode in was a two-seater. I sat on the passenger's side in the car alone while he went inside to get the corpse. I was already creeped out because I knew he would be sliding a cool stiff body in the back of the van in any minute.

About ten minutes later, I heard the back double doors to the van open. I jumped when he rolled the body covered with a white sheet and strapped down on a stretcher into the van. There were no dividers between the front and the back of the van, so I could see that he had slid the body close to me in my peripheral. When Kelvin climbed back into the driver seat of the car, he laughed. He could see by the look on my face that I was totally weirded out. I didn't accompany him for many of those rides.

He wore a huge grin on his face when he told me he got offered a job at Frito-Lay. I was proud of him for doing what he had promised me he would do, which was make an honest living. Everything was going well for us.

He moved up quickly to a lead position at Frito-Lay. The best perk about him having that job aside from the paychecks and the benefits was the free snacks he would bring home. If any packaging was damaged, they would allow the employees to take it since they could not be sold.

He boasted about every raise he received and the accolades management gave him for his hard work and dedication to the job, which is why it was extremely perplexing to me when he got arrested after getting caught up in a drug sting operation that drastically changed our lives.

By the time Kelvin had gotten arrested, I had had our second son, Tyrek. Our children were still very young. Tyrek was six months old, KB was now four years old, Kiaria was eight years old, and he was going to prison for the first time in his life.

He had been arrested for a few misdemeanors here and there prior to our marriage, but he had not had a felony charge until now.

He had so many traffic violations that his Class E drivers license had been revoked. He was issued a hardship with a Class D restriction that limited him to driving to and from work and for work purposes only. He was currently facing a habitual traffic offender and a drug sell charge.

There had been recent signs that something was not right and that he had been lying to me about his whereabouts.

It wasn't that long before his arrest that I had called Frito-Lay to talk to him and was told by the person who answered the phone that he was on vacation for the week. I was taken aback by that new information. He had been getting up every morning the week he was on vacation and leaving the house as if he was going to work.

So, where was Mr. Brown going every morning if he was on vacation at Frito-Lay? I wondered.

I soon found out when he asked his sister to go pick up some personal items for him. His sister and I pulled up to the old black house trimmed in yellow with burglar bars on the windows and doors. I sat in the car as she greeted a light-skinned heavyset young lady who handed her a box of his things. I do not know the contents of the box. After placing the box into her trunk, his sister got back into the car.

"Something ain't right," she said to me as she pulled away.

"What do you mean?" I asked.

She shook her head and repeated, "Something ain't right."

I didn't press the issue. She obviously didn't want to get into the middle of whatever her brother had going on. I suspected she was referring to the young lady who handed her the box. I also knew in my gut that that house was where he had been, not only when he was on vacation but other times as well.

My suspicions were validated when I went to visit him for the third time while he was still at the county jail in downtown Jacksonville.

When I showed up on one of his visitation days, I approached the uniformed clerk at the information window. I jotted my name down on the visitor's log and told the clerk who I was there to see. After tapping some information into her computer, she informed me that he currently had a visitor.

"Who is visiting him?" I asked, my brows furrowed.

"I'm sorry. I can't provide that information," she answered politely.

I had to think fast. I needed to get up there to see who was visiting him. My gut was telling me that it was the light-skinned heavyset girl from the black-and-yellow house.

With all the information I had found out after his arrest I knew the name of one of his friends who had also gotten locked up during the same sting operation. I was told how the visiting system works by another girl who I had become fast associates with since her significant other had been arrested in the drug sting as well.

The inmates weren't privy to who was coming up to see them. When they were escorted into the visiting areas by the correctional officers, they could choose to deny the visit or accept it.

I asked to visit his friend. I knew his friend would deny the visit when he saw that it was me and not his child's mother. All I wanted was to get up there to see who was visiting my man.

I stepped off the elevator to the fourth floor and was escorted into a room where there was a line of windows with stools in front of each window. Attached to each window were black phone receivers on each side—one on the visitor's side and one on the inmate's side.

There sat my incarcerated husband. He held the black receiver in his ear, as he looked into the other side of the window and grinned at the girl sitting on the other side. The girl from the black-and-yellow house.

As I approached the same window, he looked up at me. The shock of my unexpected presence swiped that grin right off his face.

"Oh, so this what we're doing?" I yelled loud enough to draw attention to the dramatic episode I was causing. I don't know if he could hear me or if my words were bouncing off the glass partition that divided us.

He stared at me—speechless. He didn't move. I couldn't read his thoughts through his blank expression.

"This what we're doing?! I repeated, not expecting an answer to my salty question. I didn't acknowledge the girl at all. She sat just as still and quiet as he did. "Okay! Okay! I see! We're done," I yelled before getting escorted out by the correctional officer.

I noticed his friend who I asked to visit had been escorted in, denied my visit and was being escorted back out.

Even after my wired behavior and the disruptive scene I caused at the correctional facility, I stayed. The automated recording requesting that I accept or decline the call from an inmate at the Duval County Correctional facility came soon after I left the jail house feeling disgusted, angry and exhausted. The shame of my performance back there had not yet hit me.

I accepted the call, I accepted his excuses, I accepted his begging, I accepted his lies. While accepting everything that came along with staying with him, I was also accepting his disrespect and denying myself the freedom I deserved to be happy and healthy.

I faithfully waited on this man for twenty-four months after finding out that he was not only selling drugs but had also cheated.

Two of the boundaries I put in place had been crossed. God had was no longer just showing me signs, he had shown me sights—truths that I could not unsee even if I had no more vision, but I was still deciding against being set free.

Everything was a mess. My husband and the father of my two children was in jail, I had just found out he was having an affair and I wrecked my Nissan Sentra on the way from the jail house that same day after a man driving a pickup truck ran a stop sign and I collided into him. Now, I didn't have a car.

The Nissan was my first manual stick shift and the first car I had ever paid off. I didn't know how to drive that car when I bought it off the lot. I decided that I would buy it and Kelvin would teach me to drive it.

We went out for a practice drive. I was getting the hang of shifting the gears smoother, but I still struggled with coming off the clutch and leveling out the gas without the car cutting off. I stopped at the light of a busy intersection. As I attempted to release the clutch and give the car's engine some gas, it cut off.

Kelvin's tolerance plummeted quickly from one hundred to zero, and he began to yell his frustrations at me about everything I was doing wrong. His patience was no longer than a five-second delay on a short wick firecracker. He had very little imperturbability when things didn't go the way he wanted them to go. His temper was explosive to say the least and it was never easy to lull him back into a rational composure.

"Don't yell at me!" I yelled back defending myself against his lack of patience. "I am learning."

"Eff this!" He opened the door and got out of the car, slammed the door and walked away, leaving me alone to figure out how to drive the car the four miles back home.

I might have jerked most of the way there, but I got home safe with the car's transmission still intact.

So now my car was a total loss and to add more lemons—for the first time in my life—I had a negative bank account. The bank was threatening to press fraud charges against me. Apparently, Kelvin had decided he would be his friend's personal check cashing store. He was cashing paychecks from his friend's corpse company through our joint bank account. They signed their paycheck over to him, and he then deposited the checks via the ATM and gave them the cash.

It wasn't until this financial tragedy that we found out that his normally financially secure and successful friend was on drugs, and the company was folding. He didn't have money in his business account to cover those paychecks he issued.

Kelvin was in jail by the time the checks had bounced, and the fraud department reached out to me. With tears, I explained to the fraud representative at the bank that I had no clue what was going on and that I was going to try to get the money to them to cover the deficiency. I assured her that I was not in any way attempting to steal money from the bank.

I was in awe of this train wreck of a life I was living. Kelvin was currently incarcerated, and his past misdeeds were still wreaking havoc on my life. I was exasperated by this entire situation. I called his friend who owned the company. He did not hesitate to take accountability for the checks. He and I met at the bank's corporate office. He arranged with the fraud department to settle the cost of the bounced checks. I lost my bank account with the credit union, but it was an incredible relief they did not press charges against me.

I was only twenty-two years old, and I had more than enough drama going on. I felt like my life was falling apart. I was learning so many lessons all at once.

Lord how was I going to turn these lemons into lemonade?

This situation was the worst hurt I had ever felt in my life. My heart literally ached, and I wanted so desperately for the pain to stop. I was in pain because I loved him, and I was hurt by his actions. I managed the emotional mess I was in by prayer, reading scriptures, support from family and friends, and by moving forward, but I was still not set free.

However, I had to take control of my life. I had children that I was responsible for.

I secured a job at JP Morgan Chase, applied to begin an associate of arts program at a community college, and applied for a Section Eight housing voucher with the Jacksonville Housing Authority.

I knew I needed to build security for my children. I could only depend on me to provide for them and myself now. I've never been ashamed of receiving housing assistance. Instead, I was thankful. I hope that no single mother who is working hard to provide stability for her children is never ashamed of receiving temporary assistance.

I've worked since I was a teenager. I was a taxpayer who has made financial contributions into a system that is meant to be a temporary solution for citizens in their time of need. For much of the time that I used the voucher, the Section Eight housing program paid only fifty dollars of my seven-hundred-dollar rent. I had to pay the rest, but I held on to the voucher just in case I ended up effected by one of the several Chase layoffs. Thankfully, I was there for eight years and never got laid off.

Kelvin was released from prison a couple of months early. It was only a short time before we separated and eventually divorced. He either tried to do right for a while or pretended to do right. Either way, his doing right was short lived. I thought if he went to church with me he could stay "changed," and we would be on a path to happily ever after.

Going to church does not change anybody who does not want to be changed. He only went to appease me. Eventually, he did not go at all.

After all he had done and after all the hurtful things I went through, I still waited for him for two years of my life. Although he was not deserving of any more chances, I gave him one time to mess up with women or even the simplest sign of any kind of involvement with drugs, and he was out of here. He was released from incarceration in 2004. In 2005 we were separated. I was officially done with the relationship soon after the separation.

My lack of interest in staying in the marriage began with my distaste for his lack of emotional intelligence. He had been gone for two years, and I saw no growth in his ability to handle conflicts. When I spoke up about something I didn't like or when we got into disagreements, he went days without talking to me. His efforts to punish me with the silent treatment were a turn off. The silent treatment can be a tortuous form of non-verbal communication and very mentally abusive.

When I divorced him, I added that to my list of what to never put up with in any relationship again right next to infidelity.

His avoidant communication style was highly agitating, but the lack of evidence that he was working a legal job was the deal breaker.

He no longer had the convenience of this friend's business to lean on since it had folded, so he picked up a few assignments through temporary job agencies. I don't know if it was difficult for him to get a stable job since he now had a felony on his record or if he just didn't try hard enough. I know how the system is designed. It is indeed flawed and can fail those who are trying to change for the better, especially people of color.

He fabricated a tall tale that he had found a job through a temporary agency with graveyard shift hours. He was home sleeping during the day while I was at work. He was at "work" at night when the kids and I were home sleeping. He spent weekends at home all day and night.

Nothing about his schedule or that he was giving me cash for the bills every week was sitting well in my spirit, especially since I had no idea where he was "working." I had grown wiser than I was two years prior. Plus, I didn't trust him as far as I could see him. I wasn't going to take his word or his cash and sit down and shut up.

I checked our phone records and saw some questionable numbers on there but couldn't put the pieces of that puzzle together just yet. When he was home on the weekends, I would wait until he was in a deep sleep, then I would sneak his flip phone into the bathroom to scroll through texts, the call log, and to listen to the voice messages.

I was putting insurmountable energy into things that I should not have had to worry about in any marriage. My husband was not being an honest man—he had not changed—and I knew it.

When I began having dreams about him selling drugs and cheating, I knew my dreams were warnings. I had dreams about him before that were spot-on with reality. I might not have taken heed of my father's warnings when he told me about his dreams seven years prior, but I sure took heed of my own.

"I am going to need you to provide me with a check stub," I finally told him.

"Ok. I will bring you one."

It no longer took a gut feeling to tell me he was lying. Preparing for his exit was getting easier by the day. I loved him but I wasn't in love with him anymore. I had been slowly emotionally detaching from the marriage. The lies were making it easier to say goodbye.

His first and only attempt to show me a paystub was a total insult to my intelligence, but he had done a lot of that, so what was new? I looked at the paper in my hand and thought, *have I been this much of a fool that this man thinks this will work?*

With all that you've read so far, you're probably thinking, *Yup.*

When I got home from work, I found a wrinkled, dirty, water-spotted personal check on my dresser. I looked at that check in disbelief. I didn't know whether to laugh, cry, or get angry. First, because this was a personal check. Then, the account owner's name was partially torn off, and the part of the name that was still there was smeared and not the least bit legible. I immediately called him.

"What is this?! Why did you leave me a personal check, and why is the name missing?!"

"They lost my check, so they had to write me a check and the check got wet, so the name came off." That dumb lie rolled off out of his mouth and across his lips effortlessly.

"This is not going to work for me. I need a check stub or a paycheck from a real company."

I knew I was not going to get what I was asking for. There were no check stubs or paychecks because there was no company who had his name on their payroll.

Where he was spending his weeknights was the next question. Honestly, I didn't even care at that point. He was about to be there every night and all day too.

I gave him one more week before I stuffed all his things into white garbage bags. I was expecting him to show up in the morning from his "graveyard shift." I went to bed, had a good night's sleep, got up the next morning, got my kids ready for school as I normally did, and I went to work.

Not long after I sat down at my desk my cell phone lit up with his name across the screen. I knew he was calling because he had come home to find his belongings ready for him to pick up and go.

I answered.

"Oh, so you packed my stuff up?" he bellowed through my cell phone.

"I told you I—"

He cut me off. "Alright, Okay, Alright!" Then he hung up.

When I got home, he and his white garbage bags were gone.

One of the things I learned about hurt in this relationship goes far above lies, deceit, and affairs. About a week after I silently told him to leave, he stopped answering my calls. He shut the boys out as if they were the ones who made the decision that his time in the relationship was up. The hurt I felt from his disregard for our children's emotional well-being provoked anguish in me that I had never felt before.

After Kelvin disappeared, the children weren't all that he abandoned. He also abandoned his financial responsibilities. He had a non-working car parked in the parking lot of the apartment complex we lived in. The finance company was calling me about his car payment being behind because the car was in my name.

Since the car was not in working condition, he had been driving a rental, which was also in my name. The day he left and for several days after, I texted him asking that he return the rental car. My texts and calls went unanswered.

It wasn't until over a week later that he returned the car—after I threatened to report him as an unauthorized driver on the rental car if he didn't return it.

I was glad he returned the car, but what would have been nicer had he actually paid the balance he had accumulated for the rental. When he returned the rental, he dropped it off outside of the rental car company after business hours. The card on file—my debit card—was charged for his long-term rental.

There was not enough money in my checking account to cover the full amount of the car rental. Not only did the charge wipe out what little money I did have in my account, my bank account was now over a thousand dollars in the red.

What makes matters worse, my paycheck was scheduled to direct deposit. The negative balance ate up my entire paycheck.

He was not physically choking me, but it felt as though this man had squeezed most the oxygen out of me and left me gasping for breath—barely surviving—once again. All my attempts to reach him were unsuccessful. With no regard for how I was going to feed our children, he just disappeared.

When he eventually started spending some time with the children, it was about five months after we'd separated. I allowed them to go over to his place, that he shared with a girlfriend. After their first visit, KB came home full of news to share.

"Mama, we have a baby brother," KB told me excitedly.

"Huh?" I was confused. We had only been separated for five months. If my calculations serve me correctly, it takes longer than that to carry a child to full term.

KB repeated himself as though my rhetorical "huh" was literally meant for him to come again with that information. He followed up with his baby brother's name.

I do not know why I was shocked. It is not like he had not cheated on me before. As I drove toward home, my thoughts wondered. That one day he came home and sat next to me wrecking of cigarette smoke and some woman's strong vagina scent came back to me. When I mentioned to him that he smelled like coochie, he laughed it off, called me crazy, and went to take a shower.

I couldn't wait to get my estranged husband on the phone.

"You have a baby?" I asked him.

"No. Who told you that?"

"KB told me they have a baby brother."

"That nigga lying!"

That nigga lying echoed in my head. This was his response to our son's truth and his lie.

I took the phone from my ear, and I glared at it as if he could see me giving him an evil eye. If looks could kill through the device, he would have dropped dead instantly. I hung up. There was nothing else to say.

God has a perfect timing in the way that he reveals the things we need to know. In that moment, it did not dawn on me that the woman he was living with, was the same woman I had run into a few months' prior after his disappearing act.

After Kelvin had vanished soon after our separation, I thought I spotted him driving down the highway not far from my apartment. I was driving home from work and noticed a car identical to his fly past me. As I got closer, I realized this was definitely his car by the licensed plate number. Obviously, he had gotten it fixed sometime after he returned the rental car, but the payments were still behind because the finance company was still blowing my phone up in hopes to collect their money.

"There he is," I said to myself. As I drove behind the green Pontiac Grand AM, I noticed that the person who was driving the car was a woman by the way her long reddish-brown hair flowed wildly as the wind blew through the lowered car window. I continued to follow the car for several miles.

Finally, about fifteen minutes later, she pulled the car into a parking space at a thrift store. The woman, who looked to be half black and half Hispanic, stepped out of the driver's side and proceeded to cross in front of my car walking at a steady pace toward the store.

I didn't know if this lady knew who I was and I certainly didn't know her from Eve, so I put on my nicest voice possible.

"Excuse me," I addressed her with my face sticking out of my driver's side window.

She whipped her head around and looked at me.

"Do you know that is my car you are driving?" I asked her still with the politest voice I can mustard up given the situation, keeping in mind that she could be just as clueless as I was.

"Well, you need to take that up with your husband," she spat out quickly, with her face twisted in a frown as she continued walking away.

Ouch!

That little blow below the belt confirmed an important fact, that she knew exactly who I was. I said nothing else. I drove up behind the car blocking it in.

"So, she knows who I am, and she is talking trash?" I mumbled to myself. *She also looks pregnant.*

This thought flashed in my mind briefly in the moment, but I would ask Kelvin about it later.

As I dialed the Atlantic Beach Police Department's non-emergency number, I did not feel anger. I felt somewhat in awe by her bold response and a little amused by her audacity at the same time. I reported to the officer who answered the phone that someone was driving my car and I had no idea who this person was.

She came out of the store a few minutes before the police arrived. She got into the driver side and was fuming because I refused to move my vehicle from behind—well—my vehicle.

When the officers arrived, they took my driver's license from me and ran the tag to the Grand Am to verify that the car was registered to me. She stood beside the driver's door of the car she had not long stepped out of as the officers talked to her for a few minutes before having her remove all her belongings from the car. One of the officers handed me the key chain that held the car key to the Grand AM and the rest of Kelvin's keys.

She stood with her cell phone to her ear trying to find a ride. Kelvin was not answering her calls. The heady, arrogant posture that she displayed thirty minutes earlier when I first approached her was now replaced with sunken shoulders. She looked away from me as she tried desperately to get him on the phone.

Since I promised myself transparency in this book, I cannot lie to you. With the smuggest grin plastered on my face, I made eye contact with her and let out a prideful giggle as she stood, holding her belongings in her arms, rideless and clearly annoyed. It was her hostile glare that triggered my full chuckles as I pulled off in my Mitsubishi Lancer, which I was now convinced she had taken her share of rides in with my husband—her boyfriend—and unbeknownst to me at the time, who was the father of her unborn child.

Next, I called the finance company and told them where they could find the car they were looking for. How I handled that situation might have been mean and insensitive in some people's opinions. Truthfully, I have no regrets. I approached her nicely. The situation would have gone totally different had she responded nicely.

As far as the car's repossession, I couldn't afford to take over the payments. I had my own car payments. That was a hit to my credit I had to take. I did hold Kelvin responsible for paying that debt in the divorce settlement. He never did, but he also did not pay child support either.

When Kelvin came to get his keys from me later that day, I didn't ask him directly if she was pregnant, but I did mention it.

"That girl looks pregnant," I said to him as I handed his keys out the door.

We were newly separated; he had abandoned our children, and it appears this woman might be pregnant by him. He denied any sexual involvement with her.

"I ain't messing with that girl. That's my boy D girl," he lied.

Things have a weird way of coming back around full circle. Several months later, after her baby was born and Kelvin was no longer disowning the child, I stood with my phone to my ear with a look of bewilderment on my face when this woman called me soliciting help to get rid of another women Kelvin had begun dating.

This lady was, *hmm*... How can I say this nicely? *Special*. I am not exaggerating one bit. I am assuming she got my phone number from the contacts folder in his phone.

"He is seeing this girl, and if anybody should be with him, it should be either me or you because we have kids with him, so, we need to get rid of her."

I could not believe what was coming through the speakers of my phone. I stifled a laugh. After a short pause, I finally spoke. "I don't care who he is seeing. I don't want him."

"Yes the eff you do want him," she screeched into the phone with a high-pitched voice.

As she proceeded to further curse me out, I hung up.

That whole conversation was wild. This woman was amusing to say the least. I was eager to move on from any parts of this man's drama. I was living free of his infidelities and lies and it seemed I could not escape his mess altogether. Set me free already! Lemme 'lone! There would be many more times she would curse me out.

Ironically, she would not be the only one of the women he dated that would call me. I don't know why these women thought I was their go-to liaison for him.

Eventually, the other woman that Kelvin's *special* baby mama demanded that I help her get rid of would be calling me next at one o'clock one morning looking for him after he left her stranded at work.

"He is not here, maybe he is with the woman he lives with," I told her. I hung up feeling a bit of sympathy for her before quickly settling back into my peaceful sleep. She had no idea what she had gotten herself into. Years later, she married him.

The revelation that Kelvin had been living a double life when he and I were together was revealed in the weirdest way. When those things finally came to light, I wasn't hurt or angry. I was relieved.

He even went by a totally different name. Not a name that was one letter off like *Kevin* is from *Kelvin*. His street name was Joe-Joe. At first, I was so confused when the women he was dating would call me referring to him as Joe-Joe. I had no clue who that was.

The way all the pieces of Kelvin and Joe-Joe came together is one for the books. Well, this book.

I began doing open mic poetry as a hobby after we were separated. I have a beautiful love for poetry. I have been writing poetry since I was a child. I heard there was a venue called Arielle's, not too far from my apartment where open mic poetry nights were held. I showed up one night to check it out. After a few times going to listen to others' poetry, I decided I would anxiously get on stage with my poetry journal and say what was on my mind. I became a regular at Arielle's.

One night after a poetry show, my friend Valencia and I were in the parking lot of Arielle's when a young lady approached me as I was getting in on the driver's side of my vehicle.

"Hey, I know you don't know me, but can you please take me home? I live right there." She pointed at the apartment homes behind Arielle's. "My husband doesn't want me hanging with the girl who I rode with, and he is home waiting on me."

I stood speechless and unsure about what to do. This looked too much like a hitchhiking situation. I looked at Valencia for some sign of a yes or no on her facial expression. Valencia looked back at me blanked face, not saying anything.

"Please?" The young lady pleaded. I looked at Valencia again. Still, no helpful answers were written on her face.

"Okay." I agreed to take her. "You can sit in the front."

I gave Valencia a knowing look. In my mind I was already planning a self-defense strategy. If I was going to allow a stranger in my car, Valencia was going to sit in the back and watch her every move, just in case she needed to bust her across the head if she tried something shady.

When we pulled up in front of her door, her husband got out of the red car he was sitting in, obviously waiting to see who was dropping his wife off. As he approached the car, we made eye contact. Both of us squinted, trying to see through the thick darkness who the other was.

"Nathaniel?"

"April?"

We said almost simultaneously.

His wife looked confused. "Y'all know each other?"

"This is Kelvin's wife," he told her.

Her mouth dropped open from surprise. Although he was my estranged husband's best friend and I had known him for years, I had never met his wife. This was the same best friend who years earlier, was dating Tiffany, who introduced me to Kelvin. The big city of Jacksonville was obviously smaller than it appeared.

His wife and I became fast friends that lasted for a season. A lot of the missing pieces to the puzzle about the affair with the *special* baby mama came together as we talked about everything under the sun. They were not friends, but she had gotten to know her since Kelvin brought her around.

So many unanswered questions related to the random phone numbers of certain businesses on our phone bill that I had wondered about, including the number to a visitation center where mothers whose children were in the foster care system could go to visit their children. The *special* baby mother had several children whom she had lost custody of.

The number to the hotel that repeatedly showed up on our records was where he housed her during most of her pregnancy when she had nowhere to live. So many things I wondered about began to make sense. I could have very well been set free without knowing any of that, but the more that was revealed through our conversations, the freer I felt. I didn't need confirmation that I had done the right thing by letting him go. There had been enough confirmation already given, but after letting go comes the moving on.

I promise you I am mostly a sane person. At least 99.9 percent of the time. There is that one loose screw that is not so tight that wiggles every now and then. I made an effort to be cordial with Kelvin during our separation. Time had gone by and I thought a friendship with my children's father might not be a bad idea. It was his birthday, so I invited him over for cake with the kids. He accepted the invitation to come by.

I went to the store and bought a small cake. I didn't even consider that I was taking money that could have contributed to the kids he wasn't financially supporting and spending it on him. It was a cheap cake, but nonetheless, money was spent. The kids were excited, so it was worth it.

The kids and I waited. We waited some more. He never came. I was beyond angry. You can disappoint me, but the mama bear roared when it came to my children's feelings.

Instead of using rational thinking skills and staying my behind home I wasted even more money by using gas to drive across town to his house. I took the cake I had bought and left it on his front porch with a nasty note going off about him standing my children up and what a deadbeat father he is with a butcher knife lodged dead in the middle of the cake with the handle sticking upward. Then, I got back into my car and drove home. After I thought about what I had done, I realized that I was out there acting like the *special* baby mama when I was saner than this on a typical day.

My children will probably read this and think, *Dang mama, we could have just eaten the cake.* Instead, I chose to throw away a cake and my good Family Dollar knife.

That irrational act of craziness only proved that I had a lot of emotional baggage built up that I had not yet released. It was a helpful wakeup call for me though. Oddly, after that, I did feel even freer. Some people are better off friends, but I realized there was no good in even having a friendship with him. That would even be toxic. That was the last time I made a kind gesture as a friend and a co-parent.

Divorces are expensive. Luckily, I had a legal plan with my then-job. I went to see a participating attorney and had divorce papers drawn up. The first set of papers that I had mailed to him went ignored. I had to literally chase him down to get him to sign the papers. Every time I brought them up, he either got mad or did not respond.

When I finally caught up with him, he was standing outside of one of his houses with his current girlfriend, the woman who the special baby mama wanted me to help her get rid of. As I walked up, she was walking away.

"Aren't you with someone else? Why won't you sign the papers?" I figured if I put him on the spot in front of his boo, he'd sign them.

He did. Those papers did not come to me without a small paper cut though.

"Give 'em here," He snarled.

The papers lightly sliced my finger as he snatched them from my hand. He angrily turned the pages as if he wanted them to feel his wrath because the pages themselves had personally asked him for the divorce. He flipped to the signature page and quickly scribbled his signature.

I couldn't understand why he was mad. We hadn't been together for some time and had obviously moved on. He didn't have to try and live one life with me anymore and keep the life he really wanted to live hidden from me. He was free too.

I wasn't mad when he threw the papers at me after he signed them. I caught them up against my face, proudly walked back to my car and drove off, watching my past get left behind in the rearview mirror. Owning my well-earned paper cut.

Next, I had to be able to afford the filing fee. It took me a while before I had extra money to submit the paperwork. He did not show up to the court date. I did not care as long as his absence didn't stop the process. The judge stamped the papers, and I walked out of the Duval County Courthouse legally, set free. By the time our divorce was final, I had been legally married to Kelvin for seven years.

He was not one hundred present to blame for the hurts I experienced. I saw red flags. I ignored them. That's on me.

I had to take accountability for my choices. Accountability moved my healing process along a bit faster. MEA Culpa! I chose him. When I realized that the relationship was not going to work, there was nothing I could go back to and change about my choices or what happened in the past. I made the choice to not only date but also begin what I intended to be a life-long commitment with a man who was doing things that I did not approve of from the beginning. I made a choice to marry a man that God didn't prepare for me. The worst part is that I expected him to change who he was to be with me. Change will only come from one's own heart.

I could say that I was young. I was, but I also had many warnings and several older people in my life who gave me sound advice.

It's human nature to want to place all the blame on the people who did the things that hurt us when many times we make choices that put us in the position to be hurt. Am I responsible for Kelvin's actions? No. I am not. He was wrong in several ways, but I am responsible for my own actions and choices. I chose to get in too deep with a man who gave off several red flags from the beginning. Every time I stayed with him after he hurt me, that was my choice. When I took him back after he got arrested and had an affair, that was also my choice. I chose to love him. Unfortunately, after the love came hurt.

This chapter is not meant to be a Kelvin-bashing chapter. It expresses the way I experienced him and how those experiences shaped me in good ways and in some ways that I had to unlearn. They taught me so much about myself, life, and relationships and about taking accountability for my choices.

I do not believe that any person is all good or all bad. He is a good person in many ways. He just wasn't good for me. He deserved to be with someone who he could be his authentic self with. Someone he didn't have to hide his true self from. If street life fit into who he was, then he needed someone who was okay with that. As much as he wasn't right for me, neither was I right for him.

I don't hate him and never have. I could have very easily been his friend and co-parented with peace—if he had chosen to be a co-parent. Everything that was between us in our relationship had nothing to do with our children and has been forgiven. It was how he treated my children afterwards that made all the difference in how I saw him as a person outside of our relationship.

When he and his wife slapped my son in the face by naming their adopted child his full name as he did not already exist as a junior, I didn't have any ounce of cordial left in me to converse with him about anything.

KB was a young adult, but this age didn't change the impact his father's poor decision making had on him. He was extremely hurt by his actions. Naturally, I was angry because my son was hurt. I think the slap in the face came across harder because Kelvin wasn't an active father. He had not spoken to the boys in only God knows how long and certainly had not financially supported them. Now to add insult to injury, the one thing that our son took pride in that attached him to his father was no longer special to him.

Even after Kelvin's lack of commitment as a father, KB still loved him. Every time he talked about making it big, he included Kelvin in the list of people he was going to financially bless. After the distasteful situation with the naming of their adopted son, KB barely mentions him at all anymore.

"Dang, I really don't exist to him," KB told me.

After deciding that I would not allow the bad experiences I had in one relationship to ruin love for me and realizing there is power in accountability, I was set free.

Regardless of all the challenges that this relationship brought into my life, God never left me. He was there through every storm. He protected me. He kept me sane. The worst did not happen.

My mom taught me this quote that she was taught by her mother:

"The Lord works in a mysterious way, His wonders to perform. Plant his footsteps in the sea and rides upon every storm."

This quote by William Cowper is the mood for my entire experience with Kelvin, or should I say Joe-Joe.

Three
LOVE AFTER HURT

"Love makes your soul crawl out from
its hiding place."
—Zora Neale Hurston

Ohhhhh, but there is a God! HALLEJUAH! Cue the praise music! Let me stop and do a holy praise dance! You can love again after you've been hurt.

After the hurt, there was a releasing process. I released so much bitterness and anger; and decided to forgive and allow love to come to me. That is freedom. I'm talking about a secure, safe, and healthy love. With myself first. When you are at peace and learning to love yourself, my God! It feels GOOD!

Initially, allowing myself to feel hurt, anger, disappointment, and other emotions were necessary for me to let go of my ex, but I would have been slighting myself had I hoarded those feelings and the thoughts that produced them.

LOVE AFTER HURT

Love is something we feel but also something we do. Releasing is an action. We must show ourselves even more love than we expect from others. One way to show ourselves love is to release the things that are harmful to our mind, soul, and body. To hold on to those things is a choice.

The best thing I could have done for myself was to learn to love myself and to let go of the idea of someone loving me who was incapable of giving it. Letting go meant grieving and walking away. I grieved not only for the loss of the relationship but letting go of the idea of what I desired for us to have.

Although it hurts to walk away from things and people we are emotionally tied to and the grieving process that comes along with letting go is not easy, we will reap the benefits of freeing ourselves from trying to force a type of love and behavior from someone who is not ready or able to give to us what our worth requires. Whew Chile—the abundance of blessings I secured were unimaginable.

After my relationship with my ex was over, I did not miraculously become this healed person who immediately found myself. I had plenty of soul searching to do and I still made mistakes in the dating process. I had never dated as an adult. I dated as a teenager and got married when I was nineteen. There was plenty more to learn about loving myself, loving others, relationships and life in general.

The first person that I was interested in I made sure I ruined any chance of us being together. My insecurities were still fresh and unprocessed. I wasn't ready for anything serious yet.

I used to see him come in and out of his apartment through my open blinds. He was a tall, chocolate man with full lips, a small sexy gap between his two front teeth and big, gorgeous eyes. Very easy on my eyes.

I was in the parking lot getting something from my car when I saw him going to his car.

"Where are you going?" I flirted.

One thing about me, I am not shy to speak to anyone. In today's urban dictionary, it's called *shooting my shot*.

"To the store." He smiled.

"Bring me something back." I grinned back.

"What do you want?"

"A juice."

"What kind?"

"Surprise me."

"Alright." The blushing on his handsome face showed me that he was amused and probably a little taken aback by my boldness.

About twenty minutes later, he knocked on my door and handed me a Tropicana juice.

That was the beginning of what started off as a beautiful friendship. We talked a lot; he lived right next door so seeing each other was easy. We both wrote poetry that we shared with each other.

He would come and tap on my bedroom window after the kids were asleep just to come lie on the floor next to my bed while we talked until we fell asleep. It was nice. He was nice.

The niceness was a little scary for me, but I tried my best to push my insecurities back down in my gut. On one occasion, our late-night talk session turned into a make-out session, but he stopped himself seconds later and pulled out and away, "We can't do this."

He quickly left my room and my apartment. From the conversations we had, I knew he was pacing himself and wanted to slow things down.

Which is why the letter I wrote to him came out of the blue and as a surprise to him. I had begun falling for him. I wrote a long letter to him letting him know how I felt, and that I thought he was only after one thing from me. The evidence of how he treated me did not match my thoughts about the latter nor did it match the insecurities that I felt, but I somehow still chose to think the worse.

He came to see me face to face about that letter. Specifically, the part accusing him of wanting only one thing from me.

"After I've opened up to you and shared some of the things I shared with you, some of the things I've been through, why would you think that?" He looked genuinely hurt. "You don't ever have to worry about that now."

With the stroke of my pen, I managed to mess up not only what I thought might have turned into a great relationship but a great friendship.

I learned a valuable life lesson. Heal first. If you do not, you run the risk of bleeding on those who didn't hurt you.

Another eye opener that I found out quickly about dating after being in my marriage is that there were plenty other Joe-Joes out there, and people who will cover for them.

Navy was one of many married guys who were out recklessly playing games that could hurt not only their wives but other women. In this story, I refer to him by the name I had his number programmed under in my phone. Many black people make up nicknames for just about anybody and program them under those names in our contact list. I am one of those people.

He was a close friend of my cousin's boyfriend. At the time, I was hanging out a lot with her, her boyfriend and a few of his family members whenever they were in town.

Navy wasn't the typical guy I would be attracted to. His bald cone-shaped head was not a turn on, but he was not a bad-looking guy. By my definition we were not dating. We spent a small amount of time together but nothing close to serious. I wasn't sitting by the phone waiting for him to call, nor was I blowing his phone up. At first, I thought, *Maybe I can like him.* After a short time of being around him and observing his mannerisms and behavior, I wasn't feeling him much and honestly any time we spent together began to feel like a huge waste of my time. It wasn't long before I decided to stop talking to him altogether. Weeks after I stopped talking to him, I found out he was married. To his son's mother.

The thing that hurt the most was not finding out that he lied to me. I didn't like him enough to be hurt by his lies, but I was disgusted, nonetheless. It was finding out and that my cousin—who I was close to and trusted—vouched for this guy and backed up his lies. She didn't play cupid between the two of us. Our hooking up had nothing to do with her, but she sure as heck knew he was married and acted as though his wife was only his baby mother.

As a matter of fact, everyone in the little circle knew this man was married—except me. He told me that he and his baby mama were not together, were in the same home temporarily but in separate rooms. My cousin backed up the story that I otherwise would not have believed. A man can tell me anything but, surely I can trust my family member's word, right?

After finding out he was married, one of the things that really blow my mind was that while I was still talking to him, her boyfriend had a birthday party that we all were invited to attend.

"He wants to invite Navy's baby mama too because she's also his friend." My cousin informed me.

I had no problem with that because I wasn't in a relationship with this man, and it was not my party to take an issue with who her boyfriend invited to his party.

At the party, there was no intimate interaction between Navy and his baby's mother that made me think they were married or together at all for that matter. So, I don't know what the terms of their marriage.

How I found out he was married was interesting to say the least. Another girl in the little circle, who also happened to be a family member of my cousin's boyfriend, told me he was married in quite a nasty and accusatory way.

She was upset with me because I took issue with my cousin for telling her about my personal business. The bit of my personal life that was being blabbed to her was totally unrelated to Navy. Which is also one of the reasons I was so taken aback by her revelation.

You were the one messing with a married man, she sent across Yahoo Messenger after confronting me about my issue with being the topic of her and my cousin's conversation.

I had no clue who she was talking about. "No, I wasn't. What are you talking about?"

That is when she spilled the beans about Navy being married. Then she insulted my character by accusing me of knowing the entire time after I told her I did not know.

I wasn't used to being involved in this type of drama in my friend circles. I hadn't been hanging out with them for a very long time. This kind of messiness was new to me.

As I processed what she said, I felt so many emotions at once. I felt hurt, shame, disappointment, betrayal and anger. One of the things I would never want to do is allow a man to use me to hurt another woman in the same way that I had been hurt by my husband.

When I questioned my cousin about it, she claimed that she didn't know he was married. This behavior was very familiar and quickly reminded me of the things I experienced with her when we were teenagers. I withdrew and distanced myself. Dating was starting off crazy.

The next lesson while dating as an adult came with the realization that it is very possible to develop deep romantic feelings for a friend without the desire of wanting a monogamous relationship.

I was friends with a guy that I knew without a shadow of a doubt I didn't want to be in a committed relationship with, would never try to and I knew I never would be. The problem was, even though I didn't want anything more, I had developed feelings for him. Initially, I did not view our hanging out as dating. Later, he told me he did.

He was good company, but I was starting to realize he wasn't that great of a friend. I had long realized that he wasn't anyone that I would want to build a future with the minute I began to get to know him. So, what was I doing? For a while I was just having fun. Then, it got old and worn out. Perhaps because I had gotten to a point where I was ready to settle down again and I knew it wouldn't be with him.

I prayed every day that God would give me the strength to cut him completely off. God removed him from my life, but not in the way I thought it would happen. I was the one who was no longer interested so, I thought I would say to him, "Yo bruh, this thing between us, whatever it is, it's over."

Well, I couldn't muster up the courage. Though we had the same understanding that we were both not interested in a relationship with each other, I thought he'd hate me.

Instead of being open with my communication, I began withdrawing or "acting funny" as he put it. He told me a few weeks before he walked away, "I can tell when I am not wanted around."

While I was at work, he texted me that he decided to go back to his ex to see if they could work things out. That was *the best* thing in my dating life to happen to me that didn't feel good. I had planned my cut-off; I was just waiting on the backbone to follow through. I was supposed to be the one walking away. Unfortunately, God doesn't always do the things we ask him to do the way we want Him to do them.

I had been single, meaning not in a committed relationship, for three years before I began dating my current husband.

When we first began dating, I paid close attention to his words and to his actions. I realized he was the only person I dated that all had the qualities of someone I wanted to build a life with. As time moved on, he would be one of two.

The other, I could also very easily see a future with as well. He was one other very likely person who I didn't date but was getting to know that checked all the boxes on my "future husband" mental list. No one else except these two checked the green flag boxes, but for the others, huge red flags were certainly there.

I had already made a promise myself that I was going to hold firm to what I wanted, and I refused to start a committed relationship with anyone who gave off anything that I did not want to be connected to.

It wasn't just me. I had two boys to consider. Not only did I want to make sure I was with someone who could love me God's way, I wanted to make sure my boys had a father figure in their life who was good for them. They already had a poor relationship with their biological father. They didn't need two of those kinds of relationships.

I didn't always choose the best people to date, but I mean, getting to know people and deciding who to take or leave is a part of the dating process.

Regardless of who I dated for fun, I would choose wisely who I entertained a growing relationship with. The things I had gone through with my ex didn't make me frigid toward men. I did not want an icebox for a heart. I just wanted to be cautious and mindful.

When I met Boss in high school, I would have never guessed that I would marry him someday. I was in the tenth grade when I met him—he was a freshman. We didn't get to know much about each other then.

He and my cousin were friends. She attempted to play matchmaker between the two of us. We talked for about two weeks, and we never were officially boyfriend and girlfriend. Let my husband tell it, word in the hallways was that we were together, and he went along with it. I do not recall that ever happening, but he's entitled to his version of the story.

My cousin hyped me up to go to his class to get his phone number. She told me that he liked me and that he was expecting me and gave me the intel on which class he'd be in.

Between classes, I found him in the classroom she told me he would be in and hurried up to his desk.

"Give me your number, hurry up. I got to go." I rushed him trying to get to my own class on time.

I had never talked to that boy in my life and here I was approaching him for his number and rushing him to give it to me at that. Insane, right?! Don't judge me though. This is a judge free zone.

There was so much he say/she say drama that transpired between us in high school within the short time that we were talking that our friendship alone didn't make it a month.

After we began dating as adults, there was more he say/she say drama, involving one of the same people who went back and forth between us in high school with instigations, but we decided to nip that in the bud quickly. We made a pact to keep those folks far out of our business. No one was going to destroy this twice.

Sometimes people say they are trying to help you, but you can tell by how the "help" looks and the approach, if it is far from genuine or more about causing conflict.

Depending on how old you are you probably had a Myspace account or at least heard of it. That was the first social media platform I was on. I still sign into my account from time to time just to browse around and check out the super old pictures I posted nearly two decades ago.

Some of my and Boss' early relationship memories are out there on Myspace. Myspace led us back to each other. Well, truth be told, Myspace led Boss back to me. I wasn't thinking about ol' boy.

When Boss hit me up on Myspace roughly ten years after we last talked in high school, I barely remembered the fall out in 1995.

He messaged me, *Are you still mad at me?*

Mad at you about what? I was confused because I did not remember any of what happened until we started to talk about all the drama that was started between us. Then everything about that high school experience that I had suppressed came rushing back.

After we talked, I found out that he never said he wanted to be hooked up. We laughed about this high school fiasco. I learned not only did he not ask to be hooked up, but he hated being hooked up with anyone. He did not prefer to be hitched by a middleman.

We became good friends, fast. Dating him didn't cross my mind. He was in the military and stationed across the country in California. He was a divorcee just as I was. We had both gotten married at nineteen. He had one child—a daughter named Daneisha.

Occasionally, when he would visit Jacksonville, we would hang out for good conversation and laughs. His visits were rare, but we talked on the phone and messaged often. During one of his visits, he accompanied me to a museum, which was a class assignment for a course I was taking in my bachelor's degree program, then he took me to dinner.

Our friendship had a great vibe. It was easy to talk to him about anything. He was chivalrous, handsome with smooth chocolate-colored skin. I could tell by the close-ups of his headshots on Myspace that he took pride in the soft nicely formed waves that sat beautifully on his neat low haircut. He was shorter than most guys I had dated but taller than me when I wore heels so that wasn't a problem. It's not too hard for most guys to be taller than me since I am only five-two.

He was attractive in many ways but still, dating him was not in my plans. My mind and heart did not allow me to entertain the idea of us dating at the time, mainly because of the long distance. He was such a great friend, so I stayed focused on our friendship.

It was not until the summer of 2008 that our friendship took a turn. He had been stationed in Louisiana and had not returned too long from a deployment in Abu Dhabi.

I did not know he had come into town until he called me at midday.

"Hey, I am in town. You want to do lunch?"

I was at work, but I had not taken lunch yet, so I accepted, grabbed my purse, hopped on the elevator and met him at a Firehouse Subs restaurant up the street from my job.

For me, something was different about that lunch date than all the other times we'd hung out. Something in me was different. I felt lighter. Some of the dead weight I had been carrying from my past relationship with Kelvin and previous situationships while dating had fallen off.

It was like for the first time I took a good look at our friendship and then fixed my gaze on the possibility of growing more with this tender-eyed soul sitting across from me. On that day our conversations began to change. It wasn't uncommon for him to flirt a little with me from time to time, but now I was open to entertaining his freshness.

What a wonderful summer it was. I was on cloud nine. We emailed all day. We talked almost every night for hours. Often falling asleep on the phone. Almost the same as when we were platonically friends except the conversation had taken a romantic turn, and we weren't hanging up the phone until one of us knew the other had fallen asleep.

During his next trip to Jacksonville, we had a more serious conversation about dating. He told me he officially cut things off with an old friend of his that he would see when he came to Jacksonville. His intentions were to focus on us and see where our dating each other might lead.

I went to visit him; he came to visit me. We met up in Alabama and Pensacola as halfway points. The first time I met him in Alabama, we met at his dad's house. His stepmother was out of town, so I did not meet her until sometime later.

I arrived at his dad's house first. I was invited in to wait for him. As if I was not nervous enough, his dad had *the talk* with me, as if I was the man dating his daughter. He gave me the slightly nicer version of the third degree and made sure to drive home his point of what a great person his son is and how he wants what is best for him.

He speaks low so everything he said to me was just loud enough for me to hear, but I could see then how passionate he was about his son. I'm surprised he didn't have a Glock sitting on his leg to further solidify his message. His dad has become one of my favorite people in this world and so has his wife.

I will not lie, dating long distance was not easy. It got tough. There were a couple of times we almost did not make it through the struggle. At some point we were awfully close to going our separate ways.

I had a very eligible bachelor that I was friends with, and we were feeling each other heavily. Our connection was strong and instant. We met at the birthday party of someone we were both close to. That night, we danced and laughed. The energy was an energy I had never felt meeting someone for the first time.

Before I left, we exchanged numbers. He pressed his lips gently against my forehead before saying goodnight.

When I parted ways with him that night, I had no idea that energy would follow me for quite some time.

He lived out of the state, so we spent some time talking on the phone. I was honest and told him that I was in the middle of something, and I did not know which way I was going with it at that moment. At the time, I had no idea if Boss and I were coming or going but I did not want to complicate things further. Things were complicated enough in our dating life. We were in limbo.

Boss had a friend in Louisiana he was seeing before he and I began dating. They were not seriously dating. Since we were good friends before we were anything else, we already had shared many details of our personal lives with each other. I knew he considered her a good friend and a major help to him. I also knew that after considering it, he decided that he was not interested in a long-term relationship with her.

He was a single father. Having no family and just a couple of friends in Louisiana, she was the only person he had to watch his daughter while he worked over night, so she was still lingering in the background after he and I began dating. I am not going to say that was not difficult for me sometimes.

We were not technically in a committed relationship and that was the arrangements he had established for his daughter before he and I started dating so as much as I didn't like it, I went with it.

In early 2009, we decided to commit to our relationship. We had one brief breakup that lasted about two days. Being in love did not make the challenges of long distance any lighter; neither did the challenges make walking away easy. We were both on the phone together bawling our eyes out and trying to figure out if we could make our long-distance relationship work. It didn't take long before we decided that we were going to do whatever it took to make this work. My heart melted, and I succumbed to every resistance that was holding me back from going all in when my man told me, "April, I don't want to lose you."

The way my name melted off his lips in that moment had my stomach tied up in knots. I drafted a poem about nearly everything during that time in my life. The poem motivated by the warmth and butterflies I had for Boss is called *Mesmerized.*

Once we committed to making our long-distance life work, we put in the work. We tried to make sure we saw each other at least twice a month.

Earlier, I wrote about my fear of flying. I flew to Louisiana alone at least three times. The last time being after we were married. One of the scariest things I have ever done in my life was flying alone. I was obviously motivated by love. The other times I went to visit him, I packed up the boys and we drove twelve hours and stayed at least a week or two each time.

Back then, Netflix was a DVD service only. We ordered DVDs and watched TV series together while we messaged or talked on the phone about the show we were watching. We challenged each other in virtual Scrabble on our phones. We did whatever we needed to do, within reason, to stay connected and reduce the inconveniences of having a long-distance relationship.

Boss was nothing like the typical rough guys I was attracted to when I was younger. Choosing the same type of man was not going to get me different results. Call me a sapiosexual because his intelligence is one of the most attractive characteristics about him. His enormous God-driven heart penetrated so much affection. Our emotional connection was far superior to my previous relationship. This love was certainly different. It was easy to love him.

Although he was easy to love, the strength of our now well-built and highly secure relationship did not come without some challenges. It goes without saying that no relationship is going to grow without challenges but more so because love after hurt for me, was not always easy.

Even with dating here and there, I had spent months of time alone after my break from Kelvin. I had done challenging work on myself. I learned several lessons and had grown and matured. None of that meant that I was perfect—I was far from it. Nor did it mean I did not come to this relationship with a couple of handfuls of emotional baggage.

Everyone comes with baggage. I did not come into the relationship without trust issues and insecurities. I had to learn that I can trust Boss. I had to believe by his actions that he was a trustworthy man. I put my trust issues in check several times when they roared their ugly heads.

I did not want to allow my insecurities to have a negative impact on our relationship or have him suffer the consequences of my experiences with another man that had nothing to do with him. But I was alert and paying attention to how he moved and if its actions matched his words. I was honest with him about the things I was unsure of or where I lacked trust and why. He was always open to receive my vulnerability.

It wasn't until years later that I realized what my attachment style was and identified that I had some abandonment issues. My attachment style was anxious. Boss' attachment style was secure. That was one reason why what we were building together worked so well. If you know anything about attachment styles, then you know that having a partner with a secure attachment is like hitting the jackpot. Especially, if your attachment style is other than that.

Having a partner with a secure attachment helped me to become more secure in our relationship but I had to become self-aware of how, when, and why my anxiousness showed up. In addition, we came into a relationship with a solid friendship, which was the foundation of our romantic relationship.

As my gratitude grew for the soft relationship I now had, I became more patient with Boss' imperfections. Lord knows he was patient with mine.

Sometimes it takes a genuine heart on the outside looking in to shed insight into your own heart. It just so happened on a day that I was annoyed with Boss about something, I met my BFF Rineta for lunch.

While we sat across from each other chopping on our salads, I complained on and on about the thing that Boss had done to annoy me. I recently asked Rineta if she remembers the reason for my griping, she could not recall my exact dissatisfaction with him at that moment. Neither do I, but I do remember that it was something small and insignificant. Which is one reason I do not remember.

Rineta had this look on her face she gets when something is wrong or there is something on her mind to say.

She let me finish rambling before she spoke. "You are sitting here complaining about little stuff and many people would be happy to have what you have."

I looked at her with my head cocked to the side. I took a few seconds to think about what she had said and realized that she was right. I had been just complaining away and my friend was sitting across from me looking at me like she wanted to slap me into reality.

My ranting frustrated her even more because unbeknownst to me, Boss had tasked her with making me a Mother's Day gift basket. I felt bad for complaining about something so trivial, after she brought it to my attention. There is not anything wrong with venting but when the venting goes on too long it can sound unappreciative and turn into a spirit of ungratefulness. I began to be more intentional about counting my blessings and expressing more gratitude than complaints.

Not because of the basket of goodies Boss had ordered for me, not because he is perfect, not because it isn't ok to vent a frustration but because Rineta shined a light on one of my flaws that day, and I did not want that blemish to grow into a deep imperfection that would reflect negatively on my relationship.

Boss and I got married in July 2009, the day after I graduated with my second degree—my bachelor's degree in psychology.

We did not have a big lavish wedding to match our lavish love. We had a small ceremony after the church service on a Sunday at my dad's church. My mom made me a simple but beautiful flower bouquet and she set up a small dinner at her house afterwards for the immediate family. She set up a folding table in her living room and nicely decorated it just for Boss and me to enjoy our dinner sitting across from one another. She placed a bottle of non-alcoholic Welch's grape sparkling wine on the table.

I got dressed in the back of the church near the restrooms with the help of Carol, Kisa and Tip. I chose to wear a long simple tan-and-coral Baby Phat gown that I had already in my closet, with my coral Baby Phat heels and a tiara settled on top a long and wavy hairstyle.

When I opened the door to peek into a sanctuary full of people, my eyes widened when I saw several faces I did not know.

"Who are these people?" I asked no one in particular.

We did not tell many people that we were getting married. Some of my closest friends were not even invited. After the nuptials, I was introduced to people I had never seen a day in my life. I realized that my mother-in-law had a guest list of her own that neither Boss nor I was privy to.

I do not even know if we made it out of the church before Boss updated his Facebook social media status to *Married to April Brown*. I did not have time to tell my close friends who were not there that I got married. Of course, they felt some kind of way when they saw it. It was not my intention for them to find out that way. I had no idea my new husband was going to update his relationship status before our *I Do* kiss dried up on our lips. It was cute. His urgency to share with the world he was now officially taken by me, made me blush.

One of the reasons I did not tell a lot of people when we were getting married is because mostly it was not most people's business. The other reason I did not tell some of the people who I would have otherwise shared the news with is because my abandonment issues stood in the way.

We didn't have drama, we were both happy and he didn't give me a reason to believe that he was getting cold feet, but that didn't stop the thoughts I was having about being left at the altar.

Our love seemed barely believable—it seemed too good to be true. That is one obstacle that comes with love after hurt. If you are not careful, you can sabotage a good thing by irrationally thinking that it is too good to be true, like what I did with the first guy in the story I mentioned earlier in this chapter. Since then, I had worked on my self-awareness and gained more emotional intelligence. I could allow thoughts and feelings to show up without acting on them.

Some people will do things to cause friction and conflict or walk away from the things that seem too good to be true. Walking away or having some excuse for why it isn't going to work seems less painful than waiting for something bad to happen, because in their mind, something bad is going to happen eventually.

I knew I deserved a too-good-to-be-true kind of love that didn't end. I did not have to convince myself of that. I just needed to be sure he knew it too. I was not going to sabotage my good relationship. However, in my mind, was going to save myself from the embarrassment of being left at the altar by not telling many people when the nuptials would take place.

Many people knew about the engagement, just not the actual date we were getting married. Not to mention, we did change the plans and the date at the last minute. Originally, we were going to get married in the summer of 2010 on the beach.

When I returned to work as a married woman, my supervisor congratulated me but was also confused.

"Why did you not let us know you were getting married? We could have done something for you."

I was not about to tell her the real reason I didn't say anything. Then, I was embarrassed by the thought. I smiled at her. "Thank you" were the only words I could find to say.

When I shared my thoughts about being abandoned at the altar with Boss after we were married, he thought it was a little bit of a crazy thought. He looked at me with a look of confusion. "That never crossed my mind." He assured me. "I wouldn't have gotten that far if I wasn't sure."

The familiarity of someone telling me one thing and doing another made it challenging for me to fully trust in what he was saying. I had to see the actions along with the words.

Boss was heading to Korea for a twelve-month hardship tour just a few months after we got married. His follow-on duty station where he would work after he returned from Korea, was Eglin Air Force Base in Fort Walton Beach, Florida. The plan was, the kids and I would move from Jacksonville to our new home seven months ahead of Boss' return to the states.

We purchased a home twenty miles from Eglin Air Force Base. When Boss and I walked into the 2,700 square-foot four-bedroom, 2-bathroom brick home in Crestview with our realtor, I fell in love with that house the moment I saw it. The only thing I was not thrilled about was the house sat on a steeply sloped back yard, which Boss put to fun use when he slid down it on a sled one winter day when it had lightly snowed. That house itself will forever be my favorite.

That is where we blended our two families together into one. That is the home where we brought Camden—our only biological child together—home for the first time.

Even though we had been in a long-distance relationship for our whole relationship, we missed each other more when Boss was in Korea because we saw each other less often. We only saw each other once during that entire year—for a few weeks when he came home on his mid-tour.

When he returned from Korea, it felt like no time had been lost. We were just as bonded and just as in love as we were before that distance and time separated us.

We knew each other as friends and as boyfriend and girlfriend and as a long-distance married couple. Now we were a married couple living together, which is a whole other territory. We had a lot more to learn, not only about each other but as co-parents. We had disagreements—minor arguments—we compromised, we adjusted.

Out of all the big adjustments we were making, believe it or not, our first big argument was over a Halloween party.

When his co-worker invited us to her Halloween party, we went out shopping for costumes. We were just as giddy as kids that were preparing to go trick or treating. This was going to be our first time dressing up and going to a Halloween party together. I went as a female Robin Hood and Boss dressed as a zombie cop.

When we got to the party, it wasn't quite jumping yet. We were two of the first to arrive, so it was easy to find a seat. We sat down at some of the first chairs we came across. I get along easy with most people I meet, but I am mostly quiet in new environments initially. I quietly observed and surveyed the room. A tall, heavy-set, short-haired Caucasian woman was sitting on the couch across from us. I assumed she lived with them or was good friends with the homeowner because a cat appeared and began climbing around her. She reached out and gently picked the cat up and found him a comfortable spot on her lap. The cat lay still and enjoyed the affectionate rubs she was giving it.

I do not like cats, but I was ok with sitting in the same room with one roaming around if it didn't come too close. My aunt's neighbor with the twin pit bulls were attacked by her two cats. I heard they scratched her up so bad that she had to get her hair shaved off. When I see cats, I vision her cats violently clawing at her patchy scalp.

Boss was in his element because these were his co-workers. He was socializing with the people who had arrived. I sat beside him while he enjoyed their conversations.

The doorbell rang. Someone walked in with a dog. I froze as the dog followed its owner and crossed in front of me. After they had passed, I relaxed a little bit.

The doorbell rang again. Another person walked in with a dog. Then another person. My eyes grew wide, and my body tensed.

"If one more person comes in here with a dog, I am leaving," I whispered to Boss.

As if the dog gods were against me, the doorbell rang again and in walks another person with another dog. This was certainly a dog-friendly party, and I was not a dog-friendly person. I wish I were. After reading the first chapter of this book, you might be able to imagine how immensely afraid I was at this point. I told Boss I would wait for him in the car—I left the party.

Not long after I had been sitting in the car, Boss came out.

"You can stay. I am fine in the car." I told him.

"I am not about to have you sitting in the car." He was agitated.

"This is embarrassing! I had to tell them we had to go check on the kids."

I was confused. I did not understand the problem since he knew about my fear of dogs. He could have told them the

\truth. I couldn't believe he was mad. I questioned his reason for being angry. The argument started there, and Boss was heated all the way home.

It was the most intense argument we had ever had, but like any other argument it passed quickly. After that argument, I needed him to hear me and really understand the magnitude of my fear. I needed him to know that if my nervous system could stand to be there at that party, I would have sat right there. I wanted to enjoy the party, but I couldn't be there. We talked it out after we were both calm and he has been nothing but supportive toward my fear of dogs since then.

That is what security looks like for me. To be able to argue but hear each other, empathize, take each other's best interests into consideration and take care of each other.

Although that was one of the dumbest arguments we ever had. It was a learning moment for us both. We both gained something from it to apply going forward in our marriage. We looked back on that night and laughed about it. I appreciate the disagreements that result in a stronger bond.

I got pregnant about two years into our marriage. I was *sick, sick*! It was the sickest I had ever been during any of my three pregnancies, and it was my first high-risk pregnancy. The doctors kept saying it was because it was my third pregnancy and I was older.

I was put on bedrest for the first four months of my pregnancy and was instructed by my doctor to do absolutely nothing but go to use the bathroom and shower. Boss had to drive me to all my doctor's appointments, which were weekly for a while. We had no family in the city we lived in, and it was tough for both of us.

Right before my doctor placed me on bedrest, we thought I had miscarried the baby. I passed a huge blood clot.

Panicked, I yelled out frantically for Boss to come to the bathroom. I wanted him to see what I was seeing.

We both stared at what we were afraid might be the end of my pregnancy. Neither of us knew much about what it looked like to miscarry or what we were looking at as we stood over the toilet. All I knew for sure was that I needed to go to the hospital.

While I was getting dressed, Boss had removed the clot from the toilet and placed it inside of a Ziploc bag.

At the hospital, Boss sat at my bedside just as anxious as I was as we waited to find out if we were facing the dreaded news our pregnancy had failed.

We did not wait long before the doctor joined us. She looked closely at the contents of the bag that Boss had handed to the nurse when we were first settled in the room.

Stone-faced, she spoke in a monotone voice. "More than likely you have had a miscarriage. I am going to send you for ultrasound to make sure." She jotted down notes. Without making eye contact, she continued to speak with the same emotionless tone. "This is the end of my shift. Another doctor will be in shortly," she informed us before exiting the room.

Her lack of bedside manners was not something I had the mental compacity to pour what little energy I had left into. It was common for people of color to experience that kind of treatment in the area we were living in. I felt like my world might be falling apart. The last thing I needed was for a doctor with so little empathy to treat me during this crisis. I was glad her shift was over.

The melancholy was heavy in the room as Boss and I sat, hands tightly intertwined as we waited for the technician who had a gentler bedside manner than the doctor. He walked in and introduced himself, verified who I was by my name and date of birth, and informed us that he would be taking us to get an ultrasound.

He released the locks on the wheels to the hospital bed and pushed me down the hall and around the corner. When we entered the room; he locked the wheels into place and prepared the ultrasound.

As I lay back on the hospital bed with my arms up and resting my hands behind my head, I winced as the technician spread the cold thick ultrasound gel across my abdomen with the white corded probe he held in his hand. As he gently probed around on my belly for signs of life in my womb, I searched his face for any signs that might indicate if my baby was alive. I knew he could not tell me anything but could only report his findings back to the doctor. I could not see the screen, but Boss watched the screen every second for any signs of a heartbeat. When he released a short sob, I could not tell if it was a cry of relief or of grief. Thankfully, it was a cry of relief.

All the weight of our household fell on Boss while I was on bedrest with extreme morning sickness all day and night. If nothing else showed me that he had my back, he loved me and that he was committed to me, it was the way he took care of me, the children, and the household during those four months that I could not. This was my kind of love.

This experience was nothing like the cold shoulder I had gotten in my previous marriage during my need for comfort the night my dad got sick on the pulpit and was rushed to the hospital. After being hurt, this love was healing.

During some of the time I was bound to the bed, I was mean, miserable, in an emotional crisis, and I felt like I was mentally going crazy from being in the house all day every day, and on top of all that, I was concerned about the well-being of our un-born child.

Some of the simplest things set me off. If our marriage survived my craziness during the first trimester of my pregnancy, it would last a lifetime. I was most miserable because I could not stomach the smell of most foods enough to even get it into my mouth. When I did find a food I could eat, my stomach would not hold it, and I regurgitated it all back up until all I had left to vomit up was acid.

On top of that misery, I was secluded from everyone in the house and confined to our bedroom. My senses were so heightened that any light scent sent me into another vomiting frenzy, so I stayed in the room.

One evening as I sat alone and ostracized from my family, I could hear them in the living room talking, playing games and laughing heartily. I called out to Boss to come here. Surely, he can take a break from their family time and bring me something to drink.

About one minute went by and he didn't respond. I called out to him again. This time becoming annoyed.

"I'm coming," he yelled back loud enough for me to hear him.

Another minute went by. Sixty whole freakin' seconds! Now my body temperature was getting hot. I was fired up inside and that destructive temper that lies dormant in my amygdala 99.9 percent of the time was waking up.

He is ignoring me, I thought.

The feelings of abandonment were dancing around with anger, and the thoughts that he did not care about me were hyping them up.

Another minute went by, and any little piece of rationale that was trying to settle down my emotions was lost. All the careful consideration I had for my fragile state was gone for a moment.

I got out of the bed, grabbed my favorite blue baseball bat that I kept beside my bed, walked to the ironing board that was set up in the corner and I beat up that ironing board with the bat. Like a crazy lady, I went ham, clanking the ironing board with hit after hit.

I welled on the ironing board as if it was the reason that I could only hold down chicken with A.1. Sauce. As if it was the reason that I was socially removed from everyone and everything, like it was its fault that I was stuck looking at the four sea-green walls of my bedroom twenty-four hours a day and that my normally active body had been idle for weeks. I kept clanking that bat down as if it was the reason that my husband did not make it to my side in less than the two-minute time frame that I wanted him to, because what is more important than me?

The ironing board was catching those clanks because my precious children and wonderful husband had a nerve to be up there laughing and having a great time while I sat in my miserable bed of unstable hormones.

When Boss saw the ironing board laying over on the floor on its side, he quietly picked it up and stood it back on its rocky legs. My children did not know I beat up that ironing board until they were adults and I told them.

Recently, while on memory lane, Boss and I were laughing about this ironing board incident.

"I felt sorry for you that night," he told me.

"Well why didn't you say something instead of just picking up the ironing board?" I asked.

"Because you were holding a bat."

I cracked up laughing.

I still have the bat, but the ironing board did not make it. I laugh at the memory of how I tortured and abused that ironing board. I just blame the pregnancy because it makes me seem less insane.

"Get dressed, I am taking you out," Boss told me once my bedrest order was lifted by my doctor.

After four whole months of being confined, I was finally able to leave the house and go somewhere other than the doctor's office. I had no idea where we were going. He said it was a surprise. I did not care if we went to Burger King. I could finally eat without it racing back up my esophagus.

He took me on an hour-and-a-half drive to Biloxi, Mississippi, to an all-you-can-eat buffet at a casino. I loved him even more for thinking of me in such a kind way. He had not done anything fun in a while either. We both needed it. These types of gestures are the kind things he does.

Boss often told me, "I just like to see you smile." Now more often he tells me, "I want you to be happy." Well, that makes the two of us because I want to see me happy too, but I also want to see him happy just as much. I don't buy into the popular saying, "Happy wife, happy life." I like, "Happy spouse, happy house" better. I do not get joy out of my spouse being miserable so that I can be happy. That is no way to live. There is enough happiness to go around.

Boss and I have an easy marriage. It is not perfect. We do have challenges. We disagree, and we argue. The disagreements and arguments are necessary for our growth and to maintain our voices about our own wants, needs, thoughts, and feelings. However, the arguments are not long-lasting; we still care for each other even when we are not seeing eye to eye. We are intentional about creating a safe space for one another to feel comfortable being open and honest.

I've been called a liar for saying that our life together is easy. Boss and I put plenty of work into maintaining a happy and harmonious relationship, but it isn't hard. The challenges we have faced in our marriage have never been detrimental. Every union is different and not comparable to the next. Our truth is ours alone. So is how we experience each other. Work is work. How we choose to do the work and how we think about it can determine if we view it as easy or hard. There hasn't been a time since we were engaged that we've been on "bad terms." When we disagree, we are still on good terms. One of the things I am proud of is that we do not ignore each other. The toxic silent treatment is not something we have ever welcomed into our communication styles.

In my relationship experiences, most hardships were created. There was plenty of drama in my previous marriage that made things harder than it should have been. Hardships that could have been avoided. That was a hard marriage. If we choose to create or bring drama into our lives that could potentially destroy what we have, then we will be creating situations that will be arduous to overcome. There are enough things that will happen out of our control that we will have to conquer as a team. We do not need to add to it.

Even though maintaining happiness and peace in our home is not a struggle for us, we are still learning and growing. We will always be learning and growing. Working on being better people, in general, also helps us to be better people to each other.

Since the time I have been writing this book, Boss and I got into an argument one morning. The argument lasted for about twenty minutes and the communication during that argument was off. There was no yelling, but initially our best communication skills must have gotten lost in the whirlwind of emotions because for the first ten minutes we were irrational, and we were getting nowhere; the last ten minutes were more rational and levelheaded. It is like that sometimes.

We walked away from the conversation still somewhat in our feelings with some processing to do. We gave each other our regular kiss before parting ways to start our day, and we said our *I love yous*. An hour later we were on the phone talking about something totally unrelated to the argument and our day moved on.

Communication is important, but it is not the only important thing that relationships need when there is a disagreement. It is how you repair after the argument. This tidbit I not only learned from experience but also has been proven to work though the research of one of my favorite relationship experts, John M. Gottman. *The Seven Principles for*

APRIL Y. JONES

Making a Marriage Work by Gottman and author Nan Silver is one of my favorite marital books.

Some of the strong characteristics that our relationship possesses are compassion, patience and support. The things that are important to both of us, like spiritual, financial, mental, physical, and emotional support are all present. So is our compassion because we understand that those might not look the same all the time—depending on the day. We do not deny or hide our love from each other contingent upon our ability to show up the same every day.

Our relationship does not carry a fifty-fifty rule. It is not always one hundred-one hundred either. Whatever our best is that day, or sometimes just in a moment, is our one hundred percent. The amount of energy we have available to pour into ourselves at a point in time may not even be plentiful. If we are struggling with giving to ourselves, there will not be much coming out of us to give to each other. Either of us may be giving more—or less—at any given time. The important thing is that we show up with love, understanding, and with patience.

Not many things are important enough to take precedence over either one of our mental or physical health. Compassion, patience, and support such as this was something that came new to me with this different love experience.

By walking away from a painful and hurtful situation and myself up to love again, I gained a partnership above anything I could have ever imagined. I did not deny myself a new and different experience. I freely opened myself up to a deeply intimate relationship after I had been hurt. Neither did I begin to hold back how I genuinely give my heart. I am still

LOVE AFTER HURT

myself—a more mature and better version of myself but nonetheless, I still love just as hard as I did twenty years ago. The difference is, I chose a different type of person to devote my life to. I chose someone who is capable of loving me back in the same capacity. It is an exchange of affection and commitment that is not one sided, but instead one that is equally shared. It feels good to be equally yoked and to find true love after hurt.

APRIL Y. JONES

Mesmerized
By April Brown

Hey babe…you got me mesmerized. You make me wanna love you no matter how far the distance, and it doesn't matter where you are cuz, our love travels far.
Far enough for our hearts to meet and our minds to greet each other's passions.
Passionate is my thoughts as I dream of you, trying hard to pull you out of my sleep as I awake.
As I awake and become fully aware that you're not really there I whisper thanks to God just for your presence gracing my thoughts
Thoughts of you and me, baby, you got me mesmerized. You make me wanna face my fears of flying and catch a flight one way to spend every day with you,
With you I reject all boundaries
I'm wide open and I was hoping that you too are mesmerized by me, so together we can raise the waters and part the sea that separates us,
Separates us from holding each other in the midst of storms and everyday norms, baby, you got me mesmerized.
You make me wanna be with you forever and never leave but cleave to you like Will and Jada are inseparable.
In a lifelong partnership that's unbreakable.
Unbreakable and irreplaceable, cuz you got my heart making beats that I never heard before, my eyes seeing visions that I never saw before, my tongue speaking words that I never spoke, like,
Heriberto, te extraño, te necesito, te quiero.
Baby, you got me,
Mesmerized

Four
BLOOD IS THICKER THAN WATER. SO?

"Relatives are the people you're related
to by blood, and family consists of the
people who offer you a sense of
belonging, acceptance, and connection."
—Nedra Tawwab

If I was given a dollar every time I heard someone say "Blood is thicker than water" in comparison to being blood related versus not, I would be rich. This saying insinuates that blood relatives are priority over those who are not related. Is blood thicker than water?

For me, that does not does not apply. I no longer place anyone as a priority over myself or anyone else simply because they are a blood relative. Being blood relatives certainly does not automatically make us tighter than other important relationships.

It took me a long time, many letdowns and heartbreaks to learn that just because someone is a blood-related relative does not mean that loyalty and honesty will come along with that. I am now set free from that narrative, which can leave many people in a bind and feeling obligated to people that misuse and abuse them. That was my experience many times over.

I have a plethora of relatives but as I got older, I decided for myself who I would consider family. I have many people in my life who I consider family who are not blood related and several people who are blood related who do not act like family at all. That is okay. That means that I am just a relative to them, as they are to me.

I have learned to hold on tight to those in my life who express positive and genuine feelings toward me and not focus on those who do not. It is a great peace when you do not dwell on what or who you do not have and pour into what and who you do have.

The characteristics of family resemble love, kindness, support, loyalty, honesty, forgiveness, security, people who bring out the best in you, cohesiveness, respect, and people you can feel safe around. Family may be defined differently for others. For me, it represents all those things and more.

Even though it can be emotionally disruptive, it can also be healthy for us to release the idea that just because someone is a blood relative that they are going to have our best interest at heart. It is not realistic to think that solely because someone is a blood relative means that they will handle you with care and respect or that they will stand firmly behind you no matter what. Their loyalty may lie elsewhere but maybe not with you.

My former godmother is a first cousin on my father's side. When I was a child, I would spend time over at her and her husband's home often. After she and my former godfather had their first child, which happened to be a girl, he said to me, "I have my own daughter now. I don't need you anymore."

I was standing outside of church, and the service had not been long over. I let it slide and did not say a word to my parents about it. I kept my hurt feelings to myself. Even after those harsh and harmful words I still visited just the same.

As an adult, I began to look back on that moment. I thought, *What a horrible thing to say to a child—to anyone.*

That was his doing and not my godmother's. She was still one of the kindest and sweetest people in my life through my experiences with her. Unfortunately, my experiences with her after I became an adult were a lot different. The day I released my title as their goddaughter was several years later. My then-godmother sat on the couch in my aunt's living room at a family function. It had been a long while since I had spoken to her, not for any specific reason—just life and neither of us taking the time to keep in touch.

Still a newlywed, I approached her with Boss and my wedding picture lighting up on my phone. All smiles, I attempted to show her the picture.

"I got married!" I said with excitement, extending the phone toward her.

She turned her head up and away barely looking at the picture.

"Umm hmm. To your cousin's best friend." She stated my cousin's name. Her passive response paused me.

The only other time I had experienced this type of passive-aggressive response from her was when I told her I was marrying Kelvin. I can understand her negative response to that. Not a soul I knew was happy about me marrying him, but this was different.

She didn't look back my way, did not even whisper congratulations or anything close to it. I knew then, that my cousin who she erroneously referred to as my husband's best friend—her niece—had been negatively discussing me, again. That part did not surprise me because that was nothing new.

My cousin and I had an on-again, off-again strained relationship since high school so anything she said about me was expected. What surprised me was my godmother's behavior. Although we had not kept in touch with each other regularly, I thought our relationship was still a decent one. I had no idea she had any hard feelings toward me. That moment reflected those feelings.

After that, I decided then that I did not need a mother figure in my life who chose to form a perception of me based on gossip or how someone else felt about me. It didn't matter about the hearsay; I had done nothing to her personally. Her response was all I needed to decide these were not the type of godparents I wanted. These were my relatives, but I didn't feel like I was their family.

Removing the title from a person who does not stay true to it by their actions is sometimes the most freedom you will need from the situation and the people attached to it.

Initially I was disappointed by her behavior, but I quickly moved on. My emotions had become just as much detached from the situation as their title as my godparents was by the time others were telling me negative things that she had said about me to them. All still based on what someone else told her. At that point it had all gotten much too messy. I had already removed the title, so I didn't see a reason to give the gossiping much time or energy.

Either way, they are still my relatives. That fact remains true. We can choose to walk away from certain types of relationships with people without dragging along hard feelings. We do not have to dislike them. I love them just the same, but my perspective of their roles in my life has changed.

Blended families are a notable example of how strong family relationships can exist with people who are not blood relatives.

One of the differences between my siblings and I is that I am the only one of all of us who was raised with both biological parents in the home for my entire childhood. While we were in the same home, I didn't see much of a difference in our upbringing, but their experiences are certainly their own, just as mine belong to me.

First, my early childhood home consisted of my two sisters, Carol and Angela, and one of my brothers, Tony. They are all my mother's children. My sisters moved out as, Chris and Rob, my brothers from my father's previous marriage, moved in. By that time, I was about eight years old.

I am blood related to all of my siblings, but some of my siblings are step-siblings to each other. However, that factor does not determine the strength of their relationship with each other. I do not refer to any of my siblings as half siblings. My siblings who are not blood related do not refer to each other as step-siblings. Our relationships are not built on who has the same parents or which parent we share.

My parents referred to all my siblings as "my son" or "my daughter." I did not hear the word *stepchild* in our home growing up. Unless they knew my parents before they got together, many people did not know that we did not all share the same parents biologically.

My upbringing in my blended family set the example of inclusion for how I also interact with my bonus children. I did not draw a line between them and my biological children when it came to the way I showed them love and even discipline.

Our blended family extended out to far more than just inside of the confounds of our home. I have a big extended family. Some include those who married into the family but are now divorced. In our family, divorce does not mean cutting off relationships with family members solely because someone's marriage did not work out.

Mother—my paternal grandmother—lived in a huge two-story duplex multi-family home in downtown Jacksonville. Several friends of the family and family members rented space there. Before moving in with us, my brothers lived there with their mother, although she and my father were no longer together.

BLOOD IS THICKER THAN WATER. SO?

My brothers' mom would spoil me like I was her own whenever I visited my grandmother's house. All my memories of her are pleasant, and I can only remember her treating me with love and kindness. Despite her and my father's divorce, she was family.

For the most part, our immediate family is rather close knit, give or take a few people. There have been several breakups within our family unit, but also several relationships maintained after those divorces. I can understand how unorthodox that can appear to some people. It might not always be the most comfortable situation when new romantic relationships are built, and new people come into our family because not everyone has the same beliefs that exes still belong a part of a family that they are no longer tied to through marriage.

Though it is the most important to those in it, the marital relationship is not the only relationship in a family that matters. I find it selfish to expect family members to break bonds with those people they are closely knit to because a marriage did not survive. Everyone's situation is different and some more complex, so I can understand exceptions based on the circumstances.

After Kelvin and I divorced, the bond between Kiaria and I did not disappear simply because I divorced her father; neither did it alter my decision to allow Kiaria to move in with me for a short time. When her mother asked me if Kiaria could temporarily live with me so that she could attend a particular school on my side of town, I did not hesitate with my yes. I was happy to have her there. She would always be my child. She would live with me during the week and go to her mom's house on the weekends. Kelvin was not involved much with any of the three children at that time. We were just two moms working together for a child that we both loved.

Boss was also from a blended family but with different dynamics than mine. Now here we were blending into our own family. With our differences and our similarities.

When we began our blended family journey together, KB was eleven, Tyrek had just turned eight and Daneisha was nine years old.

Boss immediately stepped into his father role. He was not just a "father figure" to KB and Tyrek; he was the only father that took care of them mentally, emotionally, physically, and financially. I love the gratitude I have seen them show to Boss for his fathering and love. It made my heart smile when they would always list his legal name—Herbert Jones—whenever they were filling out anything that would acknowledge their dad. These are the small gestures that show the person who stepped in and poured into you that you appreciate them, blood related or not.

For the first six months that Boss was in Korea, Daneisha lived with her mom in California. When Boss asked me if she could come live with me during the second half of his tour, I had no problem with it. She was my bonus daughter. Why not?

From the beginning, she was welcomed into my family with love and open arms. My parents became her Granny and Papa, my siblings became her aunts and uncles, my nieces and nephews became her cousins. She formed close knit relationships with some of them. Her relationships with some of my family members became her closest family relationships. They bonded with her quite naturally. My children received the same love and acceptance from Boss' family as well. The beauty of this was that our children were surrounded by more love.

While I know that everyone's childhood examples are not the same, it is hard for me to wrap my head around the fact that so many stepparents chose not to treat their bonus children as their own. When I talk about treating them as your own, I mean with time and attention, equally providing, bonding, showing them love, boundary setting, and being consistent.

While each situation is unique and there are circumstances that could affect the relationship the stepparent desires to nurture with the child, I am specifically speaking toward situations where stepparents just choose not to. The ones with the "that's not my child" mentality. There is not a drop of my blood that runs through the veins of my bonus daughters, but they are still my children and the love I have for them is real.

There are people I am not related to who have given me a healthier and more welcoming sense of family than some of my blood relatives. I have friends who have become my family, some of which I have created a sister bond with. You may not be able to choose your relatives, but you can choose your family.

One of the most important lessons that I learned the hard way in life is that I am not obligated to defend or be loyal to someone just because they are my relatives and because they are my relatives, does not mean that they will be loyal to me.

Learning that I do not need to compromise my character and integrity in the name of loyalty to family or anyone, began when I was a teenager. It became worth so much value to me as I got older. It took me getting into some trouble a few times to start changing my mind set about becoming involved in drama simply because someone is my family.

Some of the trouble I got into was no one's fault but mine because I allowed myself into some bad situations. I do not blame the troublemaker for my decisions to get involved in the trouble.

When I was in high school, a sophomore to be exact, I got into more trouble over my cousin's fights than I care to admit but this is my story and I'm keeping it real. Not because I was someone who liked to pick fights, or a mean person, or even a bully. It was because I felt obligated to defend and protect a family member. One whom I loved deeply.

She was really a good-hearted person, but she had a lot of familial issues going on at the time. Perhaps taking her frustrations out on others or trying to prove her toughness was her way of coping. Her trauma responses. For whatever her reasons, she chose to pick fights or instigate them. A lot. Sometimes with random people. She created situations to start fights about.

I spent my entire ninth-grade school year with no drama and no fights. My cousin joined me at Raines High as a freshman during my sophomore year. The first girl she decided to fight was over some rumors.

A few boys hung out at our house with me and my brothers regularly. One of them stole a pair of panties from my bedroom.

During this time, Tip was living with us temporarily while her mom's house was being remodeled after a fire destroyed it along with most of their things.

My cousin spent the night often. She and Tip weren't friends but were cordial with each other because I was close to them both. Tip would laugh when my cousin boldly and jealously reminded people that "I am her blood cousin" whenever I introduced Tip as my cousin.

The boys bombarded my bedroom. One of them, laughing—showing a full mouth of gold teeth—and holding up his heavily starched sagging pants with one hand to keep them from slipping down his legs, rummaged through a pile of dirty clothes with the other hand and snatched a pair of panties from the pile.

All three of us girls did our best to snatch them back. He quickly stuffed them into his pocket and ran out of my bedroom, through the living room and then out of the front door.

For some weird and freakish reason, he took the panties to school the next day, flashing them around.

BLOOD IS THICKER THAN WATER. SO?

One of the girls from our neighborhood allegedly started a rumor that those panties belonged to my cousin and the boy had gotten them by sleeping with her in the bathroom at school. My cousin was livid. She had every right to be.

The next morning, she was dropped off at the bus stop by her aunt and uncle—my then-godparents. When she exited the van, I could tell by the look on her face what was coming next. She waited until the van pulled away then confronted the girl.

"Why you lied on me?" She quickly walked up in the girl's face.

The girl looked confused. Right when she was about to speak, my cousin repeated her question. "Why you lied on me?"

I do not think she wanted an answer. As soon as those words left her lips for the second time, she pushed the girl backwards hard in the chest.

The fight was on. I jumped into action too.

Spreading rumors is wrong but so were we for physically attacking her. If I am being honest, I do not know if the girl ever said those things. That was what my cousin told me.

I did not think twice before I jumped in the bawl because guess what—blood is thicker than water. Everyone has done childish things as children. Not everyone's childish things include violence but unfortunately mine did. This was the one fight that I jumped into to help her. The others I was trying to break up, which went badly each time.

After that one fight, more came. They came out of nowhere and I had no idea what was about to happen when they did.

On a typical day, after getting off the bus at my stop she randomly picked a fight with another girl. This girl was sweet and quiet. I never knew her to bother anyone. I had never been clear on why she chose her to pick a fight with.

This girl was quiet, but she was prepared to defend herself.

My cousin pushed her. The girl swung and landed her fist dead in my cousin's eye.

She grabbed her eye and whaled.

"My eyeeee," She cried out in pain as she grew angry.

The girl was not about to give her a chance to compose herself. She went in to hit her again, but I stopped her. I extended my arms and stuck my hands out against her body to stop her.

She stumbled back into a bush.

I did not want to fight her, and I did not fight her. I just wanted to stop the fight. The fighting stopped.

I knew when I was summoned to the dean's office the next day I was in trouble. The girl's father came to the school and reported to the dean that we had jumped on his daughter.

Rightfully so, my cousin was suspended from the bus. Guess who else was suspended from the bus? Me.

I wish I could say that all lessons were learned, and the buck stopped there. I cannot.

My cousin's bus stop was one stop ahead of mine. This day, I got off at hers at her request. I regretted it soon after. As soon as we got off the bus, she went into bully mode.

She approached a girl who had gotten off the bus with us.

"What's that trash you were talking in class?"

I sighed and thought, *What in the world?* I was so confused as to what was going on here.

Initially, the girl continued her walk to cross the street. We walked in the same direction.

The next thing I knew, she hit the girl.

This girl rose like a bear. She might have been quiet but apparently her angry side was nothing to pick fights with. Licks were passed back and forth between the two of them. I attempted to pull my cousin back to break up the fight. She snatched back from me, angrily.

BLOOD IS THICKER THAN WATER. SO?

"Don't hold me," She screamed, balling up her fist as though she was going to hit me next.

I let her go. The last thing I wanted was to rumble with my own family in the middle of the street because if she hit me, it was on.

Somehow, they ended up farther down the street before they were fighting again. I ran toward them.

The girl had a fistful of my cousin's hair with one hand, and with the other she pounded her head. My cousin, trying her best to keep her footing, the girl yanked her head in an up-and-down motion as though she was aiming to bang it against the concrete.

Of course, I was not going to let that happen. I had already attempted to stop the fight by pulling my cousin away. That did not work. I raced toward them. I had to do something to stop this fight.

I pushed the girl back to separate them. That did not work out for me too well. Obviously, it was too hard of a push because she fell onto the ground. She sat on the asphalt and howled in pain. I felt horrible. This was not how my afternoon was supposed to go. If only I could press rewind. I would stay on that bus, get off at my stop, and go home.

I am assuming because she fell when I tried to break up the fight, the perception was that we jumped her. I can see how it could have been perceived that way. Word spread around school like a wildfire in the national forest in the middle of July.

I also think that because I did jump in to help her fight the first girl, people were thinking I knew about her plans to fight these other girls. It came out the blue for me just as it did for them. I do not even know if she planned them or if she did *eeny meeny miny moe* on the bus to see who was next.

I was exasperated. It was not my intention at all to hurt that girl. The drama had become too much for me.

Karma waited at her bus stop the next day. The girl's grown-up family members were standing at the bus stop looking wild and crazy as heck, like they were ready for a battle.

They were armed with bats and ugly scowls, which were scary enough. They did not need the bats. I looked out the bus window at the lady who lightly pounded the bat in and out of her hand as if she were thinking, *somebody's head is about to be a home run.* Obviously, these adults came ready to fight us, kids or not.

My cousin got up to exit the bus. I did not move.

A boy on the bus tried to intervene. "Don't get off the bus." He blocked my cousin by standing in front of her.

She giggled nervously. The look on her face showed concern but she tried to step past him. "Don't get off here." He did not move from in front of her. The doors to the bus closed and the bus pulled toward our next stop—my stop.

The bat-crazed people jumped in their cars and sped after the bus. When the bus stopped at my stop, they all jumped out of their car as we exited the bus. I knew then all hell was about to break out on the corner of 15th and Division Street.

The girl my cousin had fought with just the day before walked up to her with her entourage close behind her. They stood as her bodyguards as they watched the girl get her licks off my cousin, as if she hadn't gotten enough licks the day before. She got plenty. They were up there for revenge as if she were the one who had lost the fight. It must have been the fall that pissed them off the most.

Next, she approached me. I stood there. I have been a pro at running from dogs, but I was not one to run from people. She must have known that I wasn't trying to jump her that day because she approached me just to turn and walk away.

I wish I could say that was the last fight my cousin started that involved me. Not only did she strike a match and did not help put out the fire, but my brother Tony was also severely negatively impacted.

BLOOD IS THICKER THAN WATER. SO?

We were on the front porch of our house. By we, I mean, me and my cousin. My brother was in the house somewhere minding his business.

A boy attended our school was walking pass also minding his business. He was not a kind person, but still, he wasn't bothering us. My cousin decided she was going to provoke him.

She threw something at him.

In a split second he had doubled back. She ran into the house with him on her heels. He jacked her up inside our house in the foyer.

My brother Tony emerged. "Hey man, get out my house with that," he told the boy.

The boy released my cousin, turned around, and punched Tony. They leaned into each other and clutched together in a grapple.

My parents' room was right next to the foyer. The fight moved to their room and persisted. I followed the fight.

As Tony and the boy tussled in my parents' room, my cousin came out of nowhere with a knife.

"Get off of my cousin," She screamed into the room right before pointlessly throwing the knife onto my mom's dresser, backing off and disappearing.

We had a friend over who hauled tail out the back door, jumped the fence, and ran home. That boy always ran straight out the back door whenever he thought something bad was about to go down. He reminded me of Rudy's friend, Peter, on *The Cosby Show*. Peter took off every time something went wrong.

I swung blows at the boy from behind him. He turned around and pounced on me. He pinned me to the floor. Tony came behind him and went across the back of his head with my mom's curling iron, breaking it. A man appeared and snatched dude up, telling him to leave.

I followed him. As he exited the house, I snatched the hood off his starter jacket, then, I went back and grabbed the knife that my cousin had abandoned off the dresser and ran outside. There were people outside watching, including my aunt, who lived across the street. It was her yard man who broke up the fight.

Dumbly, I ran up to the boy with the knife. He just snatched it out of my hand and smirked. If he seriously wanted to hurt me, he had quite the opportunity.

My Aunt Joyce, standing behind me fussed at me, "Now April, you know not to be running out here with a knife."

My dad pulled up, I guess my aunt had paged him. The action was over. Everyone who was standing around cleared out.

"You don't need to be fighting any boys," my dad said to me as I sat on the burgundy sofa in our nicely decorated living room with the full mirror wall.

I was thinking, *but he was fighting my brother though, in our house at that.* I knew better than to talk back. I sat in silence.

You got to have your family back, right? Depending on the situation, no you do not. I do not regret having my brother's back that day, given the way it all started. What happened was not our fault.

The drama from that fight did not end there. The next day, the dude stood waiting for my brother after school at the bus stop. Since my brother was not there, I was the target.

"Why you tore my starter jacket?"

I mean dude, you were literally in my house in a full-on fight with my brother tearing up my parents' room, and you fix your lips to ask me why I tore your jacket? I did not have time to say anything before he pushed me.

A good friend of mine, Brian, who was like a brother, was being held back by some of the other boys. He was trying to defend me but obviously the boys holding him back wanted to see a big boy, go one-on-one with a small girl.

Being the Aquarius that I am, I wasn't going down without some type of fight. I swung at him. He stepped backward to avoid the hit. He pushed me again, but this time I fell to

BLOOD IS THICKER THAN WATER. SO?

the ground. The other kids stood around watching. Some laughed.

The question in my mind was, where was my cousin when all of this was going down?

She was just standing there watching. Later, her excuse was that she was in shock.

I was furious because not only did she start the fight which led to this incident, but she stood and did nothing to help. I was furious because not only did I attempt to help her in some way each time she started a fight that did not even involve me, but I had also gotten a semi-bad reputation among my peers because of it.

That was my thought process then. Now I take full responsibility. My brother and I had every right to be upset about the fight she started at our house but as for the other fights, I should not have gotten involved. Even if I had good intentions. Those were poor choices. That was on me.

As for Tony, the boy and his friends chased him for a while whenever they saw him.

The close friends I had at the time were like family. They were pretty good friends, so I had never had any hard lessons to learn at that point when it came to loyalty. I was beginning to learn more about what disloyalty looked like.

Those experiences taught me that doing certain things and allowing myself to get involved in unhealthy and unsafe situations to defend others is not always justified because "Blood is thicker than water." Someone being my blood relative does not mean that I am obligated to assist them in their mess or that they will have my back in the same way that I might have theirs.

I had several good moments and fun times with my cousin as well, so I genuinely wanted to continue a close-knit relationship with her as we became adults. Disconnections with loved ones is never easy. You might miss the good times you shared. It took me some time into my mid-twenties—after other non-violent incidents—to realize I needed to detach for a while, like the situation with the married guy, Navy.

How many times have you heard things like, "well, that's your sister" or "that's still your mother?" You might have even said that to someone before. Someone's spot in the family tree does not give them privileges to us. Neither does it give them the right to harm us and we continue to allow them the space to do so.

We should not undervalue family by any means, but we should also be careful of overvaluing relatives who are harmful to us in any way. It's okay to set ourselves and others free from the obligation of maintaining relationships with people just because they are our relatives. Not all relative relationships are healthy. We do not need to hold grudges or unforgiveness in our heart in order to maintain a healthy distance with some relatives. I am mindful that people do grow, and family relationships can be restored after change.

I am a firm believer that who we surround ourselves with will determine how soft or hard our life is. In my earlier relationship with my ex-husband my life was not as simple as it became after I left him. He was a part of my everyday life. His actions and behaviors complicated my life.

These days, I am surrounded by love. The family I have around me is simpler. Softer. Healthier. Freeing.

Five
Who the Son Sets Free Is Free Indeed

"If the Son therefore shall make you free,
ye shall be free indeed."
—John 8:36 (KJV)

Growing up in an Apostolic church meant, no pants for girls, no listening to the Blues, and no to a ton of other things, like going to the movies and celebrating Christmas. Of course, Halloween was out of the question but I'm not a big fan anyway.

Since my parents didn't allow me to listen to secular music, I didn't learn my first hip hop song until after my brothers moved in. Rob Base's "It Takes Two" was the first rap song I learned.

After I became a teenager, I bought my first CD's. Monica and Brandy were my favorites. I ordered those from Columbia House for the ten for ten cent deal. I never followed through with the promise I made to Columbia House to order CDs at full price within a certain time frame in exchange for the ten, but I did learn those entire CDs from beginning to end.

I spent a significant amount of time with my sisters after they moved out, so l learned many R&B and pop songs, but you better believe I knew more gospel songs than anything. I love gospel music, but I graciously credit my siblings for introducing some much-needed genre diversity into my life.

Angela's husband was in the military, so they were stationed away a lot. I spent most Christmases with Carol, so I did get a present or two on Christmas morning. I also went on trips up north with her to visit her then-husband's family during the holidays.

I had a few outlets to my parents' religious rules through my siblings. I spent most weekends with my sisters, but I had to be at church on Sunday morning whether my sisters were attending or not. They had to have me there one way or another, even if that meant riding with one of the elders and his wife while they loudly sang songs off-key, I had never heard, all the way to church.

Being in high school and not allowed to wear pants was tough for me. My parents allowed me to wear leggings if the shirt was long enough to cover my butt. I also wore gaucho pants, and culottes, some which were sewn by my mother. I sat and watched sometimes as she pinned material to patterns and cut them out before sliding the pieces under her sewing machine needle to form her masterpieces.

I wanted to wear jeans so bad, so I sneaked and wore them when I was in high school. I had this one flowered gaucho all-over pants jumper. Sometimes I would use that jumper to cover up the jeans I borrowed from my cousin until I got near the bus stop. She was my fashion savior a few times.

I was risking it all by sneaking and wearing those jeans. My mom used to pop up at my school randomly during my lunch period to bring me McDonald's. I never knew when she was coming. Lucky for my behind—and I mean that literally—it was never on a day that I had on jeans. If she caught me there was a good chance she would tan my hide.

I was not the only one sneaking and breaking church rules. I do not remember exactly how old I was, but I know I was very young when my Aunt Ernie sneaked and took me and my cousin, Mel, to the dollar movie.

My Aunt Ernie lived with my Uncle Eugene and Aunt Sandra. I spent a lot of time at their house hanging out with Mel when I was growing up. Although she is four years older than me, Mel and I were very close. In fact, she remains the cousin I am the closest knit to on my mother's side of the family.

After I got home from a weekend at my aunt and uncle's house, I was the big mouth who snitched and got Ernie into trouble. I announced to my mom, "we went to the movies!"

I really was just excited that I went to the movies. I did not think anyone would get mad at her. If Ernie was going to sneak little kids to the movies, she should have told us it was a secret.

She was an adult, but she is one of the youngest of my mom's siblings. She used to call me Chicken Legs and Sticks and I hated it; so now, Ernie and I were even.

We were in church a lot when I was growing up. We had Sunday school on Sunday morning, morning service and an evening service. Through the week, we had Wednesday night bible class and Friday night services. We also had choir rehearsal and other church functions on Saturdays sometimes. That was a lot of church going.

Do not get me wrong. I love that my parents raised me in church. We had some good times growing up. I have so many memories of God moving in that church. We sang, clapped, shouted, beat the tambourine while worshipping an omnipotent, omnipresent God.

On occasion, one lady in the church spoke in tongues. Whenever she did, the entire church was silent. Listening. Praying. She only knew how to speak English but when she spoke in tongues, she was clearly speaking a completely different language that did not sound made up or like gibberish. Her voice was strong, powerful, and bold as she interpreted what "Thus said the Lord."

When we were younger, we laughed, joked, and played about a lot of things during church but one thing we didn't do was play during those type of moments.

I must admit sometimes there were moments when laughter was hard to push down and keep inside.

During one worship service, the music was going. The guitarist played, the drummer drummed, and the singing was bumping. Suddenly, a lady started screaming vociferously and doing a holy dance in front of me. We called that shouting or catching the holy ghost. I was used to people catching the holy ghost, but this took me completely off guard. As I tried to hold back the laughter, my eyes watered. I was laughing both at her and at myself because of the way it startled me. I raced off to the bathroom.

Auntea Debbie and another church member, Sister Jackie, came in right behind me to check on me.

"You alright?" Auntea Debbie asked.

Holding my eye and trying to hide the tears that the laughter had produced, I said dramatically, "It's my eye!"

Auntea Debbie looked at me with a knowing look. "I know what you're doing," she said before they left me standing there, feeling both amused and embarrassed.

As an adult, I was on the praise team. As my mom puts it, I cannot hum a tune. She has jokes, but it is true. I love to sing. I sing all the time, but I just was not blessed with the vocals my mom and some of my aunts and cousins on both sides of my family have. That is okay because anybody who knows me knows that I am going to sing anyway.

My brother Chris wrote a song when we were kids that he and I sang at church. We both sounded horrible because he also cannot sing. At least the song was nicely written.

I would say the people must have let us up there to serenade or torture the church because my dad was the pastor, but that wouldn't be true. There were many people who came through there that sang and could not. The pastor apparently let anybody sing. I wonder if my singing sound good to God though. No? Maybe?

It was a nice gesture that allowed the less talented people like me to show case our efforts.

One of the most hated reasons to take the mic at church was being forced to repent in front of the congregation. It was the children who were disobedient or teenage girls who got pregnant out of wed lock who were further embarrassed by having to openly confess their transgressions to a room full of judgmental congregates, some visitors. The bias about that is I did not see one adult stand before the entire congregation to air out the details of their sordid skeletal closets non-voluntarily.

I never understood the purpose of being forced to ask others for forgiveness for something you may not even be sorry for. Apologies should be a natural expression and sincerely from the heart. Never forced.

My faith and my relationship with God mean everything to me. I would not give it up for anything. I witnessed God doing his works inside and outside of the church building.

My faith is strong today because of not only what I witnessed for others but also how I have experienced God for myself. Healing for instance. The one thing no one can take from me is my very own experiences.

The way that God has healed me will never be taken lightly.

WHO THE SON SETS FREE IS FREE INDEED

When I began having seizures, I was about five years old. My mother assumes the seizures might have started from the impact of my forehead hitting the woodgrain dashboard of my dad's station wagon when he suddenly stopped on brakes. I was riding in the front seat on my mom's lap.

My parents don't remember much about the doctor's reports. I cannot put a name on the diagnosis, so I will just call it The Shaker. I remember vividly this one night The Shaker took control of my body. The seizure started as I slept. Although my body trembled profusely, I could hear my surroundings. I could hear my mother crying and my father praying.

By the time the ambulance arrived, the seizure had subsided, and I was feeling almost back to myself but weak. My legs were wobbly, but I attempted to walk. As my legs were giving out on me, one of my sisters caught me to keep me from falling. I soon realized after experiencing another one of these episodes that my legs weren't ready for walking soon after.

I did not ride to the hospital in the ambulance. The EMTs checked me out before my parents drove me to the hospital themselves.

I cannot tell you how long it was before I was healed from The Shaker, but I remember many doctor visits and the day I sat at a table surrounded by a team of doctors and my parents, who were happy that I was being taken off the medication I was prescribed to take nightly before bed to prevent The Shaker from gasping me in its hold as I rested.

It was not on many occasions, but it was when I forgot to take the medication that it happened again.

There were nights when my mother would return home from church and wake me out of my sleep to ask if I took my medicine. Sometimes half asleep, I would hear her ask my siblings if I had taken it.

After I was taken off the medication, I never had another seizure again. Migraines took their place. Honestly, I'd rather *this* (migraines) than *that* (The Shaker). Either way, God has shown his healing mercies in my life on multiple occasions, beginning in my early childhood. Jehovah-Rapha.

The first migraine that I remember getting was after my paternal grandmother's funeral. I was twelve years old when she passed away.

My mother had left my grandmother's house where we had gathered after the funeral. She had gone home ahead of my dad and me. I was outside when I got an excruciating headache. I was on the steps that led up to the living area. A good friend of the family who would later become a member at my dad's church saw me crying.

"Bobby!" Sister Rose yelled up the stairs to my father. "Something is wrong with your baby!"

My dad and a few others came to check on me. "She's probably just hot," someone advised my dad after he came to my rescue.

My dad took me home. I felt sick to my stomach. My mom gave me pain meds and had me lay down in front of the window AC unit in her bedroom.

I did not get migraines often as a child.

At some point in my adult life migraines begin to take a toll on my occupational functioning. On too many occasions, I had to leave work early to get home and lay down in a dark room before the pain crippled me and the vomiting started.

Over-the-counter medications did not stay in my system long enough to work. I would vomit for hours. The severe pain would last for about four hours before subsiding into a dull ache. I had brain fog, fatigue and shakiness accompanied with each migraine that lasted for hours and sometimes days after the pain went away. Some episodes were so bad that I would have to go to the emergency room for fluids after uncontrollably vomiting myself into dehydration.

At one point, I was getting migraines weekly, the most was three times in one week. That only happened once.

I went to a neurologist, who sent me for an MRI before determining that there were no concerns with any tumors or anything more serious. He prescribed medications that I did not take for long. One of the side effects of the medication seemed to cause me to studder slightly and appeared to slow down my cognitive responses. I decided to stop taking the medication.

In church on a Sunday afternoon, I prayed, and I sought God in that moment for healing. I had my eyes closed, tears were flowing when suddenly my legs got too weak for me to stand. I just lay on the floor and wept. I could not move. I had felt the Spirit move several times, but never had I felt immobilized. I could hear praises from others all around me. Some in their own zoned out worship sessions, pouring out their hearts to God for their reasons and others praising God for whatever he was doing for me in the moment.

In the middle of my own worshipping, I could hear my dad on the pulpit. "There is healing going on in here." He spoke through the microphone.

I did not get migraines for several years after that. While they did come back it is sporadic, rare, and manageable. They no longer interfere with my life in such a way that they had done before.

Anybody who knows a thing or two about migraines might know just how crippling they can be and how much they can interfere with your life. I am thankful for the freedom to control migraines, instead of them having control over me. Especially to the extent that they once did.

Although I did grow up in a specific religion and I was taught very specific things, I began to develop as my own individual outside of some of those things that were inculcated. Not outside of my foundation of Jesus Christ and my faith. Jesus is my savior and will always be. He set me free long before I realized I needed to set myself free from the dictation of what others desired for me based on what they were accustomed to.

I did not visit any churches outside of the congregations we fellowshipped with until after I was in my late twenties and even more in my early thirties. I eventually visited many different churches. I decided that I enjoyed nondenominational churches, and that is what I began to prefer.

The nondenominational churches I attended aligned with the foundation of what I believe, and the atmosphere was different from what I was used to. I was drawn to the less censorious aura of the churches. Specifically, the few I frequented.

As I've gotten older, I've been better able to seek God for what he wants for me outside of what people might think. I love the freedom of being able to follow God without restraints and the pressure of other people's opinions.

While I appreciate being raised in the church, I decided to no longer hold on to some of the mindsets that I initially held on to. Not saying that anybody's mindset was wrong. Not everything is right or wrong. Some things are just about personal choice. I decided to make personal choices and personal changes.

One of the things that I chose to do differently for my family was to balance church and family. I did not want to miss out on things that were important to my children and spouse because we all must be there every time the church doors opened. God can be the *most* important to us while we also maintain other important things in our life.

I wanted to be able to take my children on vacations and my husband and I have our weekend getaways. I also want my children to understand that while assembly is important, God is with them even when they can't make it into the building because He goes beyond the church walls. He does not sit idle until we come back to the well-assembled bricks and sticks. Some of our best work for God is done outside of the edifice.

I wanted my children to have the freedom to participate in extracurricular activities without all their free time being tied up in church alone. I wanted to be able to support them in their accomplishments, even if that meant I missed a church service.

When I tried out to be a cheerleader in the ninth grade, both my sisters were in the stands cheering me on. I was appreciative of their support, but they were not my parents who were at Wednesday night bible study. I didn't make the team, but their presence would have still meant the world to me.

I felt let down by their absence. As an adult who found the courage to make my own choices about what I feel in my heart is right for my relationship with God, I now understand that they made the choices they thought was best for their relationship with God.

Family and marriage are also a Godly ministry that we must take care of and not neglect. Boss and I put God first by allowing him to lead us in building and bonding in our family and marriage. Unfortunately, many people have allowed "church" to tear those things down, in more ways than one.

My desire is to serve God without being controlled by any denomination. I want God to freely use me. For that to happen, I must be free to be used. It is not always me who can take me in the opposite direction of where God is trying to use me, it can also be others. And if it is others, and I allow it, that's on me.

One of the hardest things for so many people to do is to break free from the shame they gathered over the years from the church. I had religiously done things a certain way for so many years that it felt wrong to do anything differently, even when in my heart, I desired to be free to feel and think for myself regarding my relationship with God. To be able to say, "Okay, come on, God. It's just me and you in this relationship. Let's do this."

I found my freedom by rationalizing this notion:
There's a difference between being a God pleaser and a people pleaser. If the only reason that I am doing something is specifically because I feel forced and because of what others may think, not because I think God will be displeased, then I am not free.

Six
Everybody Has Them

"Everyone will have opinions, including you. You must learn how those opinions differ from the truth."
—April Y. Jones

"Nobody is that happy."
"She needed him more than he needed her."
"He felt sorry for her."
"She's only with him for his money."
"When he breaks up with you don't say we didn't warn you."
"He only wants to move you away to control you."

Things that made me go hmmmm!

I knew I had grown when Boss and I sat and laughed a good bit when we heard people's opinions and the rumors about our relationship. They knew more about us than we did.

We were both single parents when we got married. Neither of us had savings accounts overflowing with money but we both had money saved. We both worked and made decent money for the economy we were living in at the time. We both were renting apartments. There was no plethora of money for me to marry in to and Boss is far from controlling.

We got married for no other reasons than the fact that we loved each other, we wanted to build a life together, we treated each other with respect, and we knew we were two people who were great to each other. Our love was genuine.

The comments about our marriage were very comical to say the least. Because we knew our purpose together, comments like that went over our heads. We laughed them off and just kept being who we were. We didn't get where we are today in our relationship with the ability to maintain genuine happiness, by letting other people's assumptions and opinions get in our heads.

I learned that if you are hurting and being hurt, people will talk about you and when you are loving and being loved they will do the same.

Those people are entitled to their opinion. I am also a person with opinions that I am entitled to just like everyone else. I have several. With everything that I've experienced with people giving their two cents into my life, I begin to change how I put my own opinions out in the atmosphere. At some point during my growth journey, which will last a lifetime, I begin to desire to be a person who is less judgmental with my opinions. I don't aspire to be someone whose opinions tear down other people.

Opinions are evidence that people have their own minds.

Knowing who I am and accepting my flaws and imperfections has led me to also stop trying to change people's opinions about me. I don't have to like their opinions, but I also don't have to change their minds. Because I spent time learning myself and I know myself better than anyone else, I have embraced my truth and both the deficiencies and the strengths that come along with it.

What's cool about emotional intelligence and self-awareness is being in touch with yourself enough to not allow someone else's emotional chaos to transfer onto you and to be aware enough to know if people's opinions are motivated by your true behavior.

It's popular now for people to swap energy. I don't need to dislike someone and treat them like they treat me in order to feel better about them not liking me or their ill opinions about me.

It was not too long ago that I hated to be lied on. Lies used to grind my gears so badly. I am still on this journey so I am not completely unbothered by lies so much as I would like to be, and I still become somewhat agitated or annoyed by people's dishonesty. However, I am certainly not going to let anyone's lies dismantle my peace either. I've come a long way. There were days when I would lose sleep over opinions, especially if it were accompanied by lies.

If I try to control what people think, I am going to lose every time. If I am consumed by other's opinions of me, I am cheating myself out of peace of mind over things I cannot control.

By popular opinion, stepmothers are mean, uncaring, and they treat their stepchildren badly while giving their biological children royal treatment. The title *stepmother* carries such a nasty reputation that I don't like to use it for myself. I refer to myself as a bonus mom. That still didn't help me escape the infamy that heavily stains the original title.

It was the simplicity of being a mother to my bonus children that came easy for me. What was not easy was the criticism that comes with being a bonus mother.

Regardless of how much love I poured from my heart as a bonus mother, everything I did was going to be under scrutiny by somebody. Everyone loves when a bonus mother is buying the child things and taking them places, they love to see when she is giving warm hugs and kisses but when it comes down to discipline and setting boundaries, she becomes the "evil stepmother."

I was significantly present in both of my bonus daughters' lives. However, my roles were vastly different. Other than the school year Kiaria lived with me, she was with her mother full-time. Daniesha was with Boss and I full-time.

I was completely hands-on with every child in our house. The same motherly things I did for the boys, I did for Daniesha—and more. She required more.

Though I showed up in my mother's role for Daniesha in full capacity, I never tried to replace her mother—that would have been impossible—but I was the mother in the house.

I enjoyed our bonding moments, especially doing all the things together that we had in common. In a house full of males, she was the one person I could depend on to go shopping with, and we both fully enjoy it. Before she was old enough to go on her own and with friends, we went to get our nails done, got massages from time to time, and one of our favorite things to do on a Sunday afternoon was to cover up on the couch and watch a Lifetime movie while we talked trash about the characters' decisions throughout the entire movie. I was very consistent in her life as a parent, but we also talked like friends. We both have the gift of gab, so it was nothing for us to sit down and chat it up about her life, my life and everything in between.

Regardless of how much I poured my heart into being a loving and supportive bonus mom, our relationship was not always glitz and glam. I was also the villain in many stories. Amid conflict, mostly when rules were broken, and consequences were issued, I was the problem.

Boss and I were on the same page 99.9 percent of the time when it came to consequences for our children. Although we discussed everything concerning our house rules and consequences, I was the more observant parent. I paid more attention and saw more of what was going on behind our backs. I could certainly be overprotective at times. That had a lot to do with my discernment. On occasion, I would be awaked out of my sleep in the middle of the night with a gut feeling so strong that I would suddenly sit straight up out of my sleeping position when something was going on with one of our children. My gut was always right. This happened very rarely when it came to the boys, more often for Daneisha. Even now, I sometimes have dreams when something is off with her.

Daneisha had a lot of freedom but not so much that we weren't questioning her whereabouts and with whom. Like a typical teen, she had her moments when she tried to slick a can of oil and I had to wear my long and tall evil stepparent hat.

Boss was at work when Daneisha asked me if she could spend the night to a friend's house. I didn't know the friend or the friend's mother. I had never spoken to the lady a day in my life, neither did I know who else was in their home. I told her no. Even though she already knew the "spending the night away" rules, I still explained to her why she couldn't spend the night. I did tell her that she could go over for a couple of hours if it was ok with her dad.

I went to work later in the afternoon and didn't return home until the evening. I called Boss on my way home to check on things at the house—my usual, how's he doing and how are the kids?

"Daneisha went to spend the night at a friend's house," he updated me.

"She did what?" Immediately and quickly, I'm going from zero to hundred.

"She asked me if it was ok to go spend the night at a friend's house. She said you told her to ask me if it were ok."

I took a deep breath in and released it, but it only calmed me down one notch. "Do you know the parents?" "Did you even talk to an adult?"

"No, I thought you did."

EVERYBODY HAS THEM

Boss had been bamboozled. I was in awe at how easily he let her play him given the fact that her craftiness had been trending lately.

"Call her and tell her to come home." I was heated.

I recalled to him the actual conversation I had with our daughter hours earlier.

When Daneisha got home, she was fuming because she had to leave her friend's house.

"I don't understand why I couldn't stay if my dad told me I could go," she protested, fully aware of what the issue was.

In that story, I was the evil stepmother who didn't know how to stay in her lane and Boss was the pushover who let me tell him what to do. At least that time I had company in the parental doghouse.

Along with being a mother comes setting boundaries and issuing consequences. That's no different for a Bonus mother whose bonus children are with her fulltime.

Kids will be kids. Kids will have attitudes. Kids will talk smack about their parents. Kids will also reach for the parent they can get sympathy from when they feel wronged. That was normal.

What was extremely hard for me was to find peace from the untrue opinions and backlash I received as a bonus mother and the extent that some people might go to get what they want.

My most ludicrous experience as a bonus mother was when the Department of Children and Families showed up at my doorstep after receiving a call from Daniesha's biological mother.

The case worker sat across from me in my living room prepared to run off a list of accusations with the fingers all pointed at me. I sat with the long and tall imaginary evil stepmother's hat on, ready.

As the caseworker disclosed the contents of the report, her face was expressionless. I giggled. I almost let go of my composure and allowed myself to fall out in a laughing fit when she told me that the girl who I did *not* allow to clean the bathroom since she shared it with boys was allegedly being made to scrub the bathroom floor with a toothbrush.

By the time she had finished rattling off the other few fabricated and absurd tall tales, her face reflecting a hint of amusement, I could tell she knew just as well as I did that this was a waste of her valuable time and mine. There were things in that report that had never happened in my house. I had her confirm that she was at the right location.

Before leaving, she told me that there would not be any further investigation and that the case should be closed within thirty days. Although the cockamamy report was entertaining to say the least, I had mixed emotions. I felt the shock of her being there in the first place, to being tickled, and then infuriated.

Prior to the case worker coming to see me, she had gone to the high school. KB had been pulled out of his instructional learning time to be questioned about the contents of a bogus report. Apparently, she had already spoken directly to Daneisha as well, who told the caseworker the accusations were made up.

Contrary to what anyone might have believed, Daneisha was not Cinderella, and I was not her wicked stepmother.

This situation was eye opening for me. The other parent's opinion of me didn't have to be ones that I agreed with, but I can't say that I wasn't a little taken aback by the untruths. After a couple more times of phony reports, I was advised by the caseworker that I could file a complaint. I didn't. Instead, I used those pivotal moments as life lessons. It wasn't going to matter how much I tried to defend myself—or prove myself—there was no dodging the bullets of opinions. So, I stopped trying to defuse them.

Was I the perfect mom to any of my children? Of course not. Was I doing a great job at being a mom to each child in my home? I sure was. Even though I was a bonus parent who poured significantly into my bonus daughters my best would never be enough to stop anyone from forming their own opinions about me, true or not. With all my flaws and imperfections, one thing I was not was abusive.

My experience with being a bonus mother was the most I had ever cared so much about being negatively perceived and lied on in my life. Those experiences are what made my skin the thickest against the bruises and scars of opinions.

At first, I tried to change the way people saw me in this role. Battling other people's thoughts is like doing the windmill in the air until you're out of breath, not hitting a thing. Now you are just tired and exhausted, and nothing has changed. Some of those opinions were hurtful because my intentions were pure. For a while the hard part was accepting those opinions without trying to change the narrative of them.

I decided that I was no longer going to carry the burden of what other people thought about me and that I would continue to do the best I could as a bonus mother. That within itself was freeing.

It is not just the opinions of others that we must be mindful of. Our worst enemy can be the voice in our own heads. We can lack self-compassion; we can guilt and shame ourselves. We can be harder on ourselves with our own words than other people's opinions that we've worked so hard to free ourselves from.

I used to hate my legs. When I was a child, I got bitten up horribly by fleas. With the type of work that he does, my dad went into many yards and houses of dog owners. A couple of times, fleas cleaved to his pants legs and made their way to a new home—our home. Even to this day, little blood-sucking insects love to nibble on me. I am like a magnet for biting insects. I scratched and scratched and scratched regardless of how much my mom and brothers told me not to. I tried to remember to rub, not scratch, but the itching became unbearable. The scratching caused smooth, dark marks to set in from the sores. I had them all over my legs.

As I grew older, I was self-conscious about my legs. None of my peers said anything to me about the spots on my legs. I told myself my legs were ugly. I told myself people were looking at my legs and talking about me. If that were true, I didn't know it for sure, but I believed it.

I felt a lot more comfortable wearing clothes that covered my legs and when I wore anything short enough to expose the marks on my legs, I assumed people were staring at my legs when I walked in any room.

I began replacing the negative opinion about myself with, at "least you have legs." Every time I told myself my legs were ugly, I'd counter it with that thought. I started wearing clothing that exposed my legs even when I felt uncomfortable.

Eventually, I begin feeling more comfortable with showing my legs. It took a long time for the thought that people were looking at the spots on my legs and judging me to completely go away when I entered a room. Setting myself free from those negative thoughts wasn't something that happened over night, it took practice, and it took years.

Much like convincing myself that having scarred legs was better than having none, I have had to be intentional about convincing myself that I do not have to be perfect to be great.

I have struggled with moving forward in my purpose because I could not get the "what are people going to think?" question out of my mind. I have had to convince myself to do things that I know I am qualified to do and that perfection in any area will never happen.

One of many people's greatest plights is the infamous imposter syndrome. It has laid heavily on me like a weighted blanket many times.

EVERYBODY HAS THEM

When I am faced with imposter syndrome or self-doubt that hinders me from fulfilling a purpose or getting out of my comfort zone, I have learned to take baby steps.

I have always been self-conscious about speaking in front of groups of people. Everyone who knows me well says shyness is not one of my personality traits, and I agree with the majority on that, so it obviously isn't because I am shy. It's more about, *what if I mispronounce a word? Are people going to want to hear me? will they think I don't know what I am talking about? Do I know what I am talking about? will I do a good job? Will they like what I am saying?* Or *am I good enough for this?*

On occasion, I've been asked to speak to groups, and I've been invited to podcast. Even though that is on my to-do list of things I desire to do more of, I had always been torn between making myself available for those things or choosing to stay inconspicuously in my comfort zone.

When I got on the stage for the first time, in my late twenties, to do open mic poetry, it felt as though I was largely stepping out of a safe place and into the wilderness. I returned to the stage many times after that, and I was nervous every time. It brought me comfort to read my poetry from my journal, instead of reciting it by memory.

Each time I tried to coerce myself to recite by memory I failed. Each time I had journal in hand.

Except one time.

I drove to a poetry show in Orlando with a friend of mine one night. From time to time, he would throw shade at me for reading my poetry instead of reciting by memory. I let his opinions get in my head, so this night, I hyped myself up to get up there without my handwritten poem, but by the time we got to the venue, I had decided against it. Then, as we were getting out of the car, he convinced me again. So, I did. I made a last-minute, unsure decision to just do it.

When my name was called, I slowly walked away from the table where I left my light pink poetry journal sitting. I can imagine if my journal had a voice, it would have been calling my name to "please don't do this" and to "take me with you or you're going to regret it."

Ignoring my gut, I moved onto the stage without what little confidence I normally held on to when I was approaching the mic. I had abandoned that confidence on the table. I stood behind the mic and before the crowd to recite by memory one of my best poems.

I butchered that thing up like a slaughtered hen. I was humiliated because I knew I did horribly. The worst part is that "my friend" talked about how bad I did to others. Our opinions about my performance were unanimous but he didn't have to agree so openly.

He was what some would call the GOAT of poetry, so his opinion weighed heavily on me. My note to self that night was to follow my own gut and do what makes me feel the most confident in a timorous situation.

Years later, after I was well settled and established into my career as a therapist, my niece called me up and asked if I could speak on Self-Care for the Caregiver, at her church to about fifty people.

There was a mini version of myself running around in my head in a full panic, screaming "Noooooo, don't make me do it" as the rational me pondered on her request.

I wanted to do her that favor, so I decided to donate my time and expertise for her.

I worked on my presentation. The night before I was so anxious that when Boss offered me some sound and knowledgeable advice by schooling me on what he does to handle his own anxiousness when it comes to public speaking, I lashed out at him.

"Knowing those things don't make me any less anxious," I spat.

Boss looked at me as if he was thinking, *Hey ma'am, I'm just trying to help.*

My opinion of myself and what others might think that kept me so anxious about speaking to this older and probably wiser crowd of parishioners was *What if I stumbled on my words or get stuck? What if I forget what I need to say? What if they think I don't know what I am talking about? What if I don't know what I am talking about? What if, what if, what if...*

I decided that it was okay to take my notes to the podium with me, as my husband had also advised me. I was glad I did. The speakers before me had their notes as well. As I read the room and observed, I began to feel calmer and more comfortable as my time up approached.

Then the woman who addressed the crowd before me touched on some of my talking points. All the confidence I had built up started down spiraling. As she spoke as if she was reading right off my notes, I was sitting there saying to myself, *Oh my goodness, I was going to say that*. The mini me in my head was about to crank up and let the anxiety take over, but I was up next, so I could not afford to allow that chick to run amuck. I told myself that I was just going to continue as I planned and as I practiced.

I got up there, and I did just that. I referred to the woman before me on her aforementioned parts of my presentation furthering those talking points. At the end of my presentation, a wave of relief and satisfaction came over me. I had done well. But then, they asked us to sit for questions. I got through the presentation, and now I am about to be put on the spot for questions? Oh boy! The anxiety played in my stomach. I felt flutters.

We sat side by side in front of the crowd paneled together. It was going well because I was just letting the other speakers jump in and answer at first—until people started asking me questions directly. Despite the anxiety, I answered the questions like the pro that I am, *in my opinion*. Pun intended.

To further fluff my confidence, several members of the church walked up to talk to me afterward, complimenting my presentation. Prior to the start of the event the coordinator had purchased a stack of my first book, *Grow On*. They gave those devotional journals as gifts, I received an unexpected monetary gift for being there, and later, I received calls from people who were referred to me for therapy. I left that event all smiles, feeling ready for the next.

Baby steps for nourishing my confidence toward public speaking consisted of continuing to recite my poetry my way instead of allowing anyone to push the notion on me that I had to be up there performing by memory. The purpose of me getting on stage was for fun and to express myself in laid back environments with peers and friends who came out to listen to me.

Baby steps for speaking engagements consisted of me speaking to a room of fifty people before I agreed to a room of one hundred people.

Still today, this area is a work in progress for me. Instead of allowing my own negative opinions and the opinions of others to control my progress, I am prepared to continue stepping out of my comfort zone and push toward my goals.

Opinions are inevitable. When you make decisions that are contrary to what others want you to do, opinions. When you do the things that make you happy, opinions. When you make mistakes, opinions. When you get it right, opinions.

One of the most freeing things about no longer letting the opinions of others control how you see yourself is that no one can shame you about your truth, which is why I can write this book without shame nor allow anyone to cause me to feel guilty because I choose to share my experiences that involve them. I can share my stories and be proud of my growth and be okay with people having their own opinions about anything they may read or hear about in this book.

Although some opinions have a negative undertone, not all of them are based on fear, hatred, jealousy and crude judgements. Opinions can be constructive and offer insight into growth in different areas of our life. Someone may give their opinion about our business. If we accept the opinions and apply them, the changes could help our business grow.

Maybe the way we show up in our relationship can change for the better after we've sat and pondered on an opinion we've open-mindedly received from our mate. Our children's opinion of us could cause us to examine ourselves as parents. We might find that considering what they have told us could be an opportunity for growth and a stronger relationship with them.

Deciding to accept an opinion should not be based on feelings of shame and guilt. Instead, it should be based on a desire to take accountability. Change should be something we do for ourselves, not simply to appease others unless pleasing someone in that regard is causing genuine happiness, progressiveness and improvement for us as well.

I've received several positive opinions from many people throughout my life. It is okay to receive positive compliments and feedback from others, but those type of opinions should not be used as validation for who we are. While I appreciate compliments and constructive criticism, those opinions should not make who I am no more than I should allow negative opinions to break who I am. It would be a major problem for my self-esteem and self-confidence to be shaped based on what others think of me.

The same people who validate me can turn right back around and invalidate me with their opinions. If my self-confidence is riding on their validation, I will be torn down by their invalidation. Autonomy best suits me. The best validation is internal validation. Finding out what makes me happy and doing more of it, fulfilling my daily purpose, practicing self-awareness of my own feelings, exercising self-compassion, and seeking growth in the areas I desire to strengthen without needing the approval of others has set me free.

When I say that I have learned to dismiss the opinions of others and what they think of me, I don't say that to suggest in any way that it was an easy process. The struggle was real. I also will never perfect it, but I can operate in self-awareness enough to be careful when allowing the opinions of others to resonate with me.

Seven
Well, Mama'nem Did It Like This

"We can't become what we need
to be by remaining what we are."
—Oprah Winfrey

Generational cycles are in every family. Certain attitudes and beliefs are instilled into each generation from the previous one. Although I do believe in generational curses, I don't like to call every cycle a generational curse because some of these learned cycles are healthy. Even some of the unhealthy cycles are not so much a curse as they are something that can easily be changed through self-awareness.

Although some are healthy and beneficial, some are not. We are living in a time now where many people recognize generational cycles for what they are and are working on themselves to break those cycles and to heal from the trauma that some of it has caused them. That is a good thing. However, there's another side to that.

Some of the ways we were shaped came from cultural ideations that were not all bad. Some of our core beliefs were built on the strong wisdom of our parents, their parents and so on. While many people experienced a cycle of trauma that was passed down through generations, some of the same people and others also gained wisdom through generational cycles.

We can appreciate the fruitful impressions that our earlier generations left on us and at the same time unlearn the unfavorable hand-me-downs.

I often hear people talk about how shameful some of the deviating attitudes and modified mannerisms of the "new generation" are. I can imagine each generation felt the same about some of the inchoate concepts of the next generation coming up after them. Eventually some of these changes became the norm.

Change is not always a bad thing. In some of my conversations with both middle aged and elderly people, I've noticed that many of them are opposed to change and stuck in their ways. For this, it is difficult for them to see any other way as being okay except their way. Some of their venting comes with a load of negativity toward the generations that came up after them and the up and coming.

One of the most crucial elements of contentment is embracing change. When we do not embrace change, our contentment suffers. Naturally some people who are not being negatively affected by particular changes will still insist on maintaining negative attitudes toward them. Regarding innocuous change, when we understand that there is more than one right way to live in this world, we can be less judgmental and critical and more accepting when change comes.

I learned some of the best things I know from my mama. My mama is a woman who possess many strengths. I credit her for my strong-mindedness. She calls it hard-headed and says I got it from my daddy. That might be partly true. I am made up of them both. I have watched both my parents give freely over the years, from the kindness of their hearts. I witnessed my mother pour so much love and effort into taking care of her brothers.

When my Uncle Charles became too sick to take care of himself, my mom spent every day for years taking care of him until he was no longer with us. I've witnessed her check in often with some of her other brothers and selflessly support them.

Being a single mother can be complicated and overwhelming. My mother helped me tremendously after my separation from my ex. For a time, I worked on the opposite side of town from where I lived, which was a good thirty-minute or more drive depending on traffic. My children got out of school before I got off work. My mom picked the boys up from school and took them home. On some days, she was preparing dinner for us when I walked in the door.

She is a caretaker and very much a nurturer. She took great care of me and my siblings when we were children and is still a dedicated mother, grandmother and great grandmother. She is a very strong presence in the lives of her grandchildren and has been their entire lives. I love that my children have been able to experience their grandmother in such an intimate way. They certainly have something special that I was not able to experience with my own grandparents.

My mother raised resilient daughters. My sisters and I have all three faced challenges that we bounced back from without allowing those things to destroy us. All three of us accepted my mother's strong and giving spirit and made it our own.

One of the qualities my mother freely owns is her strong will. This personality trait works as a strength and a weakness. It is a strength because being strong willed can equip you with the courage to be assertive, to accomplish goals and to stand up for what is right, even if you are standing alone. My mother will surely stand alone.

It can be a weakness because it is difficult for most people, including me, to turn off our strong wills in moments where flexibility is a better option than rigidity.

There are many things that I choose to carry with me from both my mother and father that I have used to develop and shape myself into who I enjoy being. Then there are those things that I found healthier for me to leave behind.

As I got older, I admired my strong-willed personality trait, but I also began to practice being more fluid. I am still finding a balance in this area. I have decided that I did not want to be stuck in some of my high-strung ways but instead be free from habits and thought processes that I do not find helpful in any parts of my life.

It is easy to become stuck in certain habits because that is how our mom, grandmother, father and other people in our village did it. None of us are exempt from toting around habits, traditions and core beliefs of the people who played a part in shaping who we are.

I often wonder if my grandmothers were around longer, what I would have taken from them and carried in my heart and mind for my lifetime and how it would have benefited me. I know they had so much greatness in them.

My maternal grandmother, Sister, passed away when I was four or five years old. I kept the memory of my mother having an emotional conversation about it in the foyer of my childhood home as I sat on the one step that led to the formal living room. I cannot recall the person's face or voice whom she conversed with as she told them the details of the events that lead to her mother's death. The emotional aura that filled the room carried a heavy sadness.

The same feelings of sorrow that lingered in the atmosphere as my mother and I—hand in hand—walked around outside the day of the funeral service. Maybe she needed some fresh air or a moment to escape the heaviness of the grief inside of those walls. However, the recollection of my mother's tears and sadness hangs around in my memories.

Since I was so young when Sister passed, I do not remember much about her. When I was a kid, I used to have dreams of Sister popping out of the hamper in my small closet wearing a Pepto Bismol-colored pink skirt suit. The memory of her in that pink suit comes from a picture of her that I saw. In the picture she was sitting on a pew inside of the church.

If I had to guess, I would say that my mother got her sense of humor from Sister because she loves to quote aphorisms, some of which she learned from Sister. She cracks me up all the time with her wittiness. She doesn't fall short of sending my children into a hearty chuckle with her quips either. We never know what she is going to say or when it will come, but we can count on her for a good laugh.

I have gotten to know Sister and what her personality may have been like a little bit from the stories my mother told me countless times.

My maternal great-grandmother, Granny, was not far from a centenarian when she passed away. She was in her late nineties. Many of our family members called her Baby and some Sugar. Before she had gotten to a place in her elderly age where she could no longer live on her own, she lived in a two-story home in a rural neighborhood known by the residents in that community as The Woods.

My mother took us out to The Woods to see Granny. My last mental picture of Granny in the house is her sitting in the living area off from the kitchen in what had to be her favorite chair. She wore a turban over her hair; a few gray hairs sprouted from her dark brown chin. We sat and laughed with her for a little while. She would always have a glob of chewed up gum pressed behind her ear. I never knew what she did with it. Maybe she chewed it later. We did not leave a visit with Granny without a stick of Juicy Fruit gum and a piece of fruit from one of her fruit trees.

Although I was a preteen when Mother, my father's mother, passed away, I can recall more of our pleasant interactions than I can conversations. Her mannerism was the sweetest and her hugs were comforting. I can imagine my father got his gentleness from his mother. From my brother Chris' perspective, as sweet as Mother was, she still didn't play or tolerate foolishness from anybody. He said she'd put you in your place with a smile on her face.

Even though I cannot remember many things specifically about my grandmothers, I can rest assured that some of the attitudes they possessed are carried out through my parents, which became a part of me and who I am today.

It's a running joke in the black community about how black grandmas and mamas didn't play about noise when it was thundering and lightning. That was my mother. When it stormed, my mom would cut out all the lights and make a pallet on the floor. We were instructed to follow suit. We had better not make a sound, answer the phone, or move around while it was lightning. Tony and I would lay on our pallets whispering. If we got too loud, we were scolded.

According to my mom, her mother covered the mirrors and made them sit down during thunderstorms since lightning strikes tall things.

My mother has been serious about her thunderstorm etiquette for as long as I can remember. She told me exactly why. When she was a teenager, her grandmother called her on the phone during a thunderstorm to get a rundown of what was in the refrigerator. She went back and forth from the refrigerator to the corded phone to tell her what she needed from the store. When she picked up the phone that last time, she heard a big boom. Lightning had struck the phone pole outside of their house. She screamed, threw the phone down, ran, and jumped into bed with her mom, who was already lying down because of the lightning.

"What's wrong with you?" her mother asked.

"The lightning hit me."

The lightning did not strike her directly, but the impact of it striking the phone pole while she held the phone to her ear was enough to make her deathly afraid of lightning.

She wasn't always afraid of lightning until then. When their mother was not home, she and her siblings bravely played outside while it was lightning.

When I became an adult and had children, I followed those shut-your-butt-up-and-sit-your-butt-down lightning rules. We turned off everything in the house and lay down during thunderstorms. We lay in bed instead of the floor. My mother's anxiety rubbed off on me. Thunderstorms scared the living daylights out of me. Still do.

After Boss and I got married, turning off everything and no movement during thunderstorms stopped. At first, I tried to implement the thunderstorm rule in the house but that isn't what he was accustomed to, and he was not afraid to watch television during a thunderstorm.

I told him, "This is what my mom had us do during thunderstorms."

He laughed as if I was being ridiculous.

I may no longer care about turning off the television and laying down still anymore during thunderstorms, but hubby had to compromise on keeping the blinds closed.

My mother did not play about us saying certain words. One of them was lying. It was perfectly normal that the word was off limits—I never wondered or questioned why as a child.

WELL. MAMA'NEM DID IT LIKE THIS

It wasn't until I had my own children that I began to question why I did not allow them to say the words *lie* or *lying*.

I questioned my own thoughts and beliefs about why my children shouldn't say them. The only thing I could come up with is because that is what I was taught by my mom when I was a kid. After much thought, I discovered that I didn't personally have an issue with my children saying those words, as long as they didn't call me a lie. If somebody was lying and they said somebody is *lying* then I mean, somebody must be lying or at least they thought they were.

I removed the restriction from my children that they were not allowed to tell me that someone was lying without having to rephrase lying to *storying or fibbing*.

I begin to gradually change my parenting to reflect more of my own mindset than my parents' and others'. Not because I thought that their way was wrong. I just decided that right or wrong, I didn't have to follow their impressions just because that is what they chose. I was free to choose based on my own logic.

When Boss and I blended our families, we had to tear down some of our own ways and create *our* way. We were raised in two totally different types of family dynamics. He had his views on parenting from how mama'nem did it, and so did I and outside of that, our own personalities.

Since Boss did not live with me and the kids right after we tied the knot, the real challenge began after his military assignment in Osan. He was finally home with us. It was an adjustment for sure. Not only were we blending our children together in the same home, we were blending our mindsets, attitudes and beliefs. Our three children had to adjust to having two parents in the household after only living with one for so long. We also had to adjust to having another parent in the household as well.

We did not struggle much with compromise because we both were open to different perspectives, but some things took longer for me. I was more rigid in some of my processes than Boss, especially when it came to some of the restrictions I had as a child that I implemented as a parent.

Halloween was one. When I was a kid, the only people we opened the door for on Halloween were our friends and we were not giving out any candy. If our kids wanted to go trick-or-treating or give out candy, Boss was all for it. I was skeptical at first because I was taught that Halloween was evil and of the devil. My compromise was as long as they didn't dress up in a costume that resembled evil or celebrate it by doing anything evil then we could allow them to participate.

The Christmas tree is also something I had never put up until our second year of marriage. All my life, I had been taught that it was against God to put up a tree in your home and decorate it because the pagans' decorated trees and worshipped them.

Now I was married to someone who did not have the same beliefs about these holidays, and he had a child whom it would not have been fair to cut off from participating in those things simply because of my long-lived perception of them.

He had allowed Daneisha to participate in these activities before we were together. We didn't want one child in the house to participate in something the other kids could not.

I thoroughly examined my thoughts, did my own research about my beliefs, prayed about it and at the end of it all, I felt good about making those changes.

If I had done my own research and I was convinced that those things would damn me and my children to hell, I wouldn't have budged, and I would have stood on what I believed. Compromises needed to be made, and the best way to do that was for us to dig deep into our beliefs and where they came from.

WELL. MAMA'NEM DID IT LIKE THIS

Blending within our home was one thing. Then there were the extended families. I was more stuck on family traditions than Boss was. Not because I just had to stick to any tradition, but more so because that is what was expected of me.

Boss and I both are from big families, and we both enjoy time with our extended family. His family has a traditional yearly family gathering. He has never committed himself to being available each time. He decides when the time comes if he's going or not. On the other hand, my family has the traditional yearly Thanksgiving gathering that I always planned for, and we were expected to show up.

My family is big on getting together. When we come together, we have a great time as we enjoy each other's presence. We talk loudly, laugh, dance and eat well. Most of the time our gatherings consist of my parents, my sisters, significant others, our children, and their children.

Boss and I both decided there were things we wanted to do differently, and we didn't want to be stuck on repeat for any holiday. We wanted to be free to decide on a whim sometimes or make plans for some of our holidays to look different from the last. We specifically outgrew the traditional splitting time between his mom and my family's house on Thanksgiving every year.

Changing that was harder for me than it was for Boss because I received backlash from my family. This was one of the things that came up in a session with my therapist. She reminded me of the things I already knew. Guilt should not be associated with family traditions, and holidays are not the only time we have to spend with our loved ones. Nor is showing up for those things the only way we can show love to our family.

I am a believer that family traditions are a great way to bond and create memories, but change should be welcomed instead of criticized. I should be comfortable moving with fluidity within the traditions. If it feels more like a stiff commitment, it isn't as enjoyable for me.

We could be so stuck in our ways or the ways of how our family decided to do things years ago and kept it going that we neglect the wants of the family we create with someone else. For some people, it works—it works for the family they created, and they are fine with sticking to what was laid out for them. If it is not working anymore, we can find what does.

Although I didn't get many spankings while I was growing up, spanking is absolutely something I had seen a lot. In my extended family and at church, having a switch off the tree to keep your children in line while in our church was so common, you would have thought it was an accessory to some of the adults' outfits, like a purse or necklace.

In church, children were supposed to sit down and sit still during service. That was the order set by the older people in the church.

There was one church member who watched the children closely. Any little movement and somebody were getting in trouble. She threatened to beat everybody's kids. Whichever parent let her, she was on it. It was like she got joy out of whopping on children.

When KB and Tyrek were small, I carried my switch accessory to church often too. There were times when I'd pop them with the switch or take them in the back by the bathrooms to at least threaten them with it. I never put welts on my children, but they did get the switch on their little legs.

In my head, this was what we were supposed to do when our children wouldn't sit still and behave well in church. This was how you showed the church members that you had control over your kids during service.

By the time I had Camden and began taking him to church, that was no longer my way of thinking. I decided that approach was unnecessary and excessive.

The church we attended had a daycare that we were able to take him in once he turned one. We tried it out a couple of times, but he would cry a lot, so we didn't make him go. When he got restless during service, either Boss or I would take him outside and let him walk around and give him a snack and something to drink before returning to the sanctuary. There was not going to be any more spanking of little children for age-appropriate behavior in our household when we could correct and guide him—and get productive results.

Through generations we have repeatedly heard, *spare the rod, spoil the child*. I do not believe that Proverbs 13:24 meant that you had to physically beat your children in order not to spoil them.

The King James Version of that scripture reads, *"He that spareth his rod hateth his son: but he that loveth him chasteneth him betimes."*

I understand that sparing the rod here means the avoidance of correction, authority, discipline, guidance and consequences. Applying those things when disciplining your child does not have to be physical punishment, or getting the butter from the duck, as our elders used to say.

My dad is from a small town in Georgia. He told me stories about how the neighbors could say they didn't speak while walking past their house, and they got a butt whipping without question. I can picture how back in those days they had a village they could trust a lot more than the so-called village we have today. But even then, the adults in the village were not always right.

We went on to discuss corporal punishment in schools. "Y'all were okay with our administration having us bend over and swat us with a paddle?" I asked him and my mom.

"Yeap" They answered in unison.

"There is something about a black child bending over while the white woman hits me with a board that just doesn't sit well with me."

"I didn't really think about that then. When we were growing up, we were in segregated schools and our parents trusted the teachers. The teachers genuinely loved the students," my dad told me.

My dad and I can converse from topic to topic seamlessly, agreeing on some things and agreeing to disagree on others.

He disagreed with some of the ways parents are parenting these days. I believe he was referring to gentle parenting. I do agree with his theory that some parents are creating entitled, disrespectful children by withholding discipline, but that is nothing new. I do not agree that all discipline needs to be physical to raise respectful, well-mannered children.

I explained to him that gentle parenting or even just parenting your child without the use of physical contact does not mean no discipline, no consequences and no boundaries.

My father has never spanked me by the way. I think he doesn't realize how much of a gentle parent he was when it came to his baby girl.

Perhaps *some* children who run wild, with no respect for their parents or anyone else for that matter may have had no consequences, a lack of discipline and boundaries, and not much guidance. There is a lot more that goes into parenting children than discipline. Sometimes key components that children need may be missing from the parent-child interactions and relationships that could result in some unwanted behaviors.

I do not have all the answers, nor do I know everything about parenting, but I do know as parents, we may overlook our own shortcomings or flaws at times. I know for a fact I have. The changes that need to be made may need to start with us, which could initiate the changes we want to see in our children.

I am not judging anyone who chooses corporal punishment as a choice to discipline their children. I know that many parents use this method. While I am not proud of some of the reasons and the way in which I used that method in the past, I was a parent who did use it as well.

Do I think I ruined my children? No, I do not, but that doesn't justify my actions that they didn't deserve. Could that have affected them in some kind of negative way? It could have.

I learned that there are other effective forms of discipline out there to consider. Eventually, I decided to choose methods outside of the norm for my family and what I learned growing up. Holding my children accountable, creating structured boundaries in our home, guiding them and disciplining them through other ways were more effective for them.

It took me a little while to get to what I call for myself, a more emotionally intelligent way of parenting. Once I became a single parent, I became harder on my boys, mainly KB. Tyrek was younger so he kind of just flew under the radar. I felt like since I was raising them alone, I had to show them that I did not play.

Whenever KB would "talk back," I would flick a quick pop to his lips. He was becoming a teenager, so those teenage attitudes were on the rise. What the older folks called, *smelling himself.* I thought that popping him on his lips made me a great mom and especially if other people saw it and thought, *wow, she doesn't play.*

My actions were also rooted in fear that if I didn't make sure they knew that I would beat them down if I had to, they would become out of control, and I would have failed as a single mother raising boys. It did not make me a bad mom. It's just that those actions are not what made me a great mom either.

I did not think to sit down and talk to him, find out if anything was bothering him or if he might have been hurting about the changes in our life that were happening to the three of us—not just to me. I am sure he was not only affected by his father's absence but also by my own emotional unavailability while I had to deal with my new normal as well. He could have felt scared. Or just having a bad day. Maybe he wasn't understanding his own emotions as he moved into the teen era of his life.

During his early teenage years, I came around to being a better listener and allowing him the space to use his voice—respectfully.

I still felt a conversation was necessary about the err in my ways because though he never brought it up, I didn't know how it affected him. He was an adult when I had an apologetic conversation with him.

"I don't think it was anything wrong with it. I think I needed that." He told me.

"No, you didn't." His response made me sad. "I don't want you to think that is how you are supposed to parent simply because that's what you saw."

It was not so much the quick pops to the lips. The epiphany for me was when I realized he wasn't being heard enough. It was more about not being quicker to listen than I was to discipline.

A voice is something I didn't see many of the parents around me give their children when I was growing up. To express themselves meant that we were "talking back," and that was disrespectful. Children just needed to be quiet, listen and do what they were told.

My parents were not necessarily the shut up and never speak your mind type of parents. Sometimes I felt I could express my thoughts, but it depended on what those thoughts were. Other times I was afraid and didn't feel comfortable going to talk to them about some important things.

I noticed the same cycle happening with my boys. I became curious about what my children had to say. I might not always agree with them, but I would take their voices in and consider what they are telling me. Teaching them how to use their voice starts at home.

I knew they would not talk to me about everything, but I wanted my children to be more comfortable expressing themselves to me and talking to me about most things. When Daneisha was a teenager, there were plenty of things she shared with me that sent a wave of shock through my body as I struggled to keep a straight face.

As a younger mother, I made a lot of parenting choices that I am not proud of. As an older and wiser mother, I've made parenting choices that I am not proud of. Most likely, I am going to make more parenting choices that I am not proud of, but I am going to continue to grow. I am going to continue to examine the choices that I make and why I am choosing the methods or techniques that I apply.

If I find that any methods that I adopted from my upbringing or what I have learned from anyone else around me work for my child in a healthy way, I will hold on to it. If I find that it does not, I will leave it.

Letting sleeping dogs lie and sweeping things under the rug is a monster of generational cycles. Family secrets have hurt more people than they have helped. So many people have found it more difficult to heal from trauma because they have been taught not to talk about it.

Too many people have suffered physical and sexual abuse and have held on to those secrets that have pounded on their consciousness for years. When they have found the courage to tell their story or confront those who hurt them, they have been met with backlash from the perpetrator and other family members. As if some survivors don't already feel enough shame from their own thoughts. I've seen this happen so much in different situations that I didn't want to tell anyone what happened to me either.

When I was a teenager, I was held down by a relative while he forced himself on top of me, fully clothed. The words *stop* and *leave me alone* were ignored. I attempted to wiggle myself free as he thrust his groin up against me. It was only when he heard someone coming that he released me. He was not much older than I was.

It was not until I was an adult that I told anybody about that incident. I didn't feel safe telling anyone when it happened—not because I thought he would hurt me, but because I did not think I could say anything and be heard. I thought I would be scolded and I thought it was partly my fault because I did not fight hard enough. I also felt ashamed that it even happened. I did not think it affected me at all for a long time.

It was not until recent years that I decided to tell a few people. Even several years later it was not easy to release those words because of the ounce of shame I still felt and because of who that person was. After the details fell from my lips, I felt relief instead of shame. It was then that I felt freed from that ugly moment.

Since the day my children were able to understand, I have tried my best to etch in their brains that they can always tell me if someone is hurting them, and at least if they are not comfortable enough to talk to me, talk to someone who can help them.

Unfortunately, some people have been taught that seeing a therapist is not necessary—to just pray about it and leave it alone. Those who believe in prayer should indeed pray about the things that they are hurting about. They should also do the necessary things to work on their healing. The necessary thing for them might be to talk about it. The decision to talk about it might be better done in a non-biased safe space.

Though we have much work ahead of us, I am proud of the amount of work that the black community has begun to do toward healing by releasing the notion that keeping trauma bottled up inside is the strong thing to do.

When I began going to therapy it helped me to open my thinking even more and increased my self-awareness. In turn, I was able to examine my thoughts and behaviors. I discovered where some of the patterns of my thinking came from but most importantly, I was able to identify unhealthy thinking patterns.

Identifying those unhealthy thinking patterns created a change in me. I desired growth. I wanted to be a better person overall—a healthier version of myself. The journey never ends. The things that we implement in our life to be better are something we practice daily. It is never complete or final while we are still on this earth. We mess up, we start over. We fall, we get back up and keep going.

As I move along, I am releasing those core beliefs that no longer serve me. As I move through change, I can shake free from the dysfunctional cycles that I thought was ok because it was my normal.

My mother was the parent who cleaned and did most of the cooking. Although my mom did work sometimes, my dad did most of the working outside of the house.

She cooked on Mondays through Thursdays. On Friday and Saturdays, they picked up take-out, and on most Sundays, we went out to eat. If we ate at home on a Sunday, my dad would cook.

She had my siblings and I do simple household chores, like hanging our clothes on the line to dry, then ironing them and put them away. To this day, I barely pick up an iron because I ironed so much then that I hate it. I honestly would rather wear wrinkled clothing but to get my bestie Kisa off my back I iron—sporadically. She has and will point out that I need to iron because my clothes look wrinkled, no matter how much I tell her that I don't care about wrinkles.

When Boss would ask me to iron his military blues, I questioned if he really loved me or if for some reason, he had grown to hate me. I should have had it written in our wedding vows that asking me to iron was grounds for a divorce.

When I became a wife, I followed my mother's cooking schedule with a slight deviation. I cooked every day except Friday and Saturday. According to the *Book of Wives* that was filed away and etched in my brain, I was prepared to fulfill all my wifely duties.

Kelvin volunteered to help clean, and I accepted. As I got older, and by the time I remarried, I no longer saw the responsibility of the household chores as just mine. In some houses, that is what works for them. In other houses, it's a generational mindset of what the wife is supposed to do.

When Boss and I got married, neither of us had the expectation that I would be solely responsible for those things, just as the impression was not that he would be the only one responsible for finances. In that aspect, we ran our home like a well-oiled machine. When I was out of work, I put more time and energy into household chores without discussion; except when I was on bedrest. When I went back to work, we shared more of the responsibilities, without discussion. Eventually, I fell off from my cooking schedule, and cooking was shared more often between Boss and me.

I was at a family gathering, and one of my aunts told me to come and fix my husband's plate from a generational mindset that since I am his wife, it is certainly my wifely duty and responsibility to do this. I am not opposed to serving my man. I do often, but my husband will also not hesitate to do the same for me. We do not see a reason to have a structured approach to serving each other. We do what is needed in that moment.

Cooking, cleaning and fixing plates are surface examples of how you might be judged as a wife by the old schoolers. There are several old generational household cycles that may not work for everyone or not everyone has to choose them to be a great spouse. I decided that generational expectations for what a traditional wife's role in the household looked like were no longer working for me mentally or physically, even though some of the ways I have decided to implement self-care is criticized. I don't know about you but some of these older generational mindsets will have me stressed out, worn out and stretched thin.

I was having a conversation with someone from the baby boomer's generation who was complaining about how people can now order their groceries at home and how lazy that concept is. There are several valid points that could easily invalidate that opinion. Personally, I have saved a tremendous amount of time and have gotten more accomplished in a day by ordering my groceries and having them delivered.

Now more families are hiring house cleaners to come in and clean their homes amid their busy schedules. They are also utilizing laundry services. These are all changes that do not affect anyone except the person who chooses to use these services and those that are getting paid for them, but somehow are still highly criticized.

I am in the number of the vast majority of women who are no longer choosing to become burn out before delegating responsibilities or outsourcing household tasks. The generational mindset that doing it all is what we are supposed to do to show strength is playing out. Especially for women.

While some old generational ways and cycles are going away with the way the world is evolving, not every change or new method is bad.

The conversations about the changes of time with my dad are the best for me.

"I've been working since I was old enough to pull a weed." His stories about his upbringing are interesting to say the least.

He worked on his family's farm. He is over eighty years old now, and he's still working way too hard in my opinion, but that is not an argument that anyone can win against him.

"Is that why you don't know how to sit down and stop working so much?" I asked him.

He laughed. "We didn't come up like the kids these days."

"With every generation it got easier," I replied as we went on to further discuss how technological growth has even made chores and other responsibilities much easier now than when he was growing up.

These things are positive and helpful changes. The one thing we can all benefit from is to embrace the changes that do not cause us harm and accept that all new generational paradigms are not detrimental or wrong.

Eight
Here's Where I Draw the Line

"Deal with yourself as an individual
worthy of respect, and make everyone
else deal with you the same way."
—Nikki Giovanni

It is clear from some of the previous stories that I struggled with boundaries earlier in my life. I had to set myself free from weak boundary setting and do what was healthy for me rather others liked it or not.

Boundaries are not a bad thing, although those who take offense to them might think so. The purpose for my boundary setting is not to keep people out of my life or to control people but rather to create a safe and healthy space for myself and others around me.

HERE'S WHERE I DRAW THE LINE

Although some people will not remain in our life due to healthy boundaries being set, it isn't because we do not want them in our life; it's mostly because they chose not to respect our boundaries, and their behavior was interfering with our life in an unhealthy way.

There was some major boundary crossing I experienced that pushed me to become more assertive and create better boundaries for myself and others. I've had to place boundaries around my marriage, my children, my business and myself.

When I set boundaries with my ex-husband, he crossed them, until I decided that I would no longer tolerate the disrespect. My boundaries did not change his behavior. They changed mine. You know the story.

When I separated myself from a family member, who I no longer felt had my best interest at heart, I was establishing a boundary for myself. I decided I would no longer hang out regularly with anyone who didn't respect me. You know the story.

I was demonstrating boundary setting then, but it wasn't until later that I became even stronger with my boundary setting and my assertiveness. There was one hurtful situation that increased my awareness of how I allowed people to treat me.

Can you imagine going to get your child from someone's house and they refused to release them to you until they were ready? My middle son, Tyrek, was about six years old when this happened to me.

After a family outing at the movies, Tyrek went over to a family member's house to play with her youngest son. In this story, I am going to call her Brenda. It was not unusual for him to spend time at Brenda's house.

After pulling out from the theater's parking lot, I thought, *Tyrek doesn't have any clothes for tonight or tomorrow.* Her son's clothes were too small for him to borrow.

I lived about five minutes from the movie theater. I called Brenda and asked if they could come down to my apartment to get Tyrek some clothes to change into after a bath and to wear the next day.

Brenda was riding in the car with her teenage daughter, who was driving. She must have answered her phone with the speaker on because when I asked Brenda if they can come get the clothes, I heard her daughter in the background give the answer to my question.

"I don't have my child," she responded curtly.

Brenda laughed at her daughter's response. "I'll just wash his clothes."

I frowned. "Okay." We hung up.

Then, I thought about that conversation for a few minutes. I will not lie, I was feeling some kind of way about Brenda's daughter's onery attitude. It was unnecessary and disrespectful. I was also disappointed that Brenda found her daughter's disrespectful attitude toward me amusing.

I would have been okay with a simple no to my request for them to come get clothes for Tyrek. I didn't understand what all the attitude was about.

I decided I would let Tyrek play for a little while and then I would go across town to their house and get him. My close friend lived over on the Westside, and I could visit her while I was out that way.

I called Brenda a few times to let her know I would come pick him up a little later. She didn't answer.

It wasn't uncommon for Brenda to ignore calls or texts, but I had an issue with her not answering my calls while my child was with her.

Now at this point, I was annoyed.

I called Brenda's husband and told him I was trying to call Brenda, but she wasn't answering the phone. He told me he didn't know why she wasn't answering her phone. I told him to let her know that I was coming to pick up Tyrek soon.

"I don't have time for people acting funny." I added.

He said, "OK."

We ended the call.

HERE'S WHERE I DRAW THE LINE

After I drove the thirty mins it took to get to their house, I called Brenda again to let her know I was outside to pick Tyrek up and to send him out. Again, No answer.

I called her husband. No answer. I called her daughter. No answer.

I called my sister, Carol, to ask if she had talked to any of them, and I explained that I was outside of their house.

"No, but let me call." We hung up, and she called.

"She said she isn't answering the door since you said she was acting funny," Carol told me when she called me back.

At this point, my blood was boiling. While I sat there, I thought about putting a brick through the window. I thought about calling the police. So many things crossed my mind. Instead of doing anything, I waited.

I sat outside for over an hour before they decided to let my son out of their house. I was beyond angry.

Something changed in me that day. The ultimate disrespect was that someone refused to release my child into my custody at my request. A major boundary was crossed. I had always looked up to her and trusted her, so I never imagined that Brenda would do something like that to me—until she did.

If that wasn't enough, she then went on social media and posted a message attempting to taunt me about not getting my way and having to teach me a lesson. She did not teach me the lesson she thought she was teaching but there was a lesson learned. A huge lesson about enforcing my boundaries. A lot of trust and respect for Brenda was lost that day. I decided that would be the last time I would let anyone push me over.

Her husband was the only one who called to offer me an apology, which he did the very next day. I don't hold grudges so of course I have long forgiven all of them, but I learned something more about respect and boundaries from that situation.

If you allow people to disrespect you and cross boundaries, they will surely do just that. People do not cross certain lines with people they respect. If they respect you, they will honor your boundaries. I highly suspect that she would not have tried that with anyone else.

After that experience, it became a lot easier for me to establish and protect my boundaries with just about everyone for a combination of reasons; it was the strength of the anger that I felt that day, the disappointment because of who it was that did this and the fact that this is the type of behavior was not healthy for my child to see.

One other thing I learned later about that situation, is even when someone you trust crosses a boundary in such an invasive way, you can grow past it and learn to trust them again, if they treat you with respect going forward.

By the time Boss and I were married my boundaries setting came easier and stronger. I came into this marriage protecting it at all costs. Establishing boundaries around our relationship was highly criticized. We were already getting hit with plenty of negative opinions regarding our boundaries.

Our marital boundaries were tested quite a bit when we were newlyweds. Some of Boss' family members had a difficult time adjusting to not being first on his list of priorities anymore. When one of his family members told us that "marriage is just a piece of paper" when she figured her wants should be priority over mine, Boss quickly defended our marriage.

Sometimes people see boundaries as an attack against them, when that isn't what a healthy boundary is at all. Our boundaries are established for us. They help us to honor each other. The most important boundary setting in our relationship started with us setting boundaries with ourselves about how we were going to respect each other and our marriage.

HERE'S WHERE I DRAW THE LINE

Months after we were married, I was preparing to move away from Jacksonville to the city where we would start our lives together. The old friend of my mine who I prayed away before Boss and I began dating, asked me to meet him for "closure." I declined the invitation. Despite my saying no, he continued to call multiple times and bombarded me with text messages. He was adamant about meeting up with me. I showed respect for my husband by standing on my no.

He wasn't the only one though. Women have a bad habit of calling other women insecure when they cannot have their way in your relationship. I planned Boss a surprise going-away dinner for family. One of his old friends with benefits was not happy that I chose not to invite her.

"You're too cool of a guy to be with someone so insecure" she advised my husband about his actual wife.

I laughed at the nerve. I had no problem with them remaining platonic friends. I just did not feel comfortable with her attending dinner with us. Her response told me everything I needed to know. I had made the right decision. Genuine friends respect marital boundaries.

We both came into the relationship with opposite-sex friends with whom we maintained communication and friendships. We have never let opposite-sex friendships interfere with the peace in our marriage. We have boundaries that we do not cross or allow others to cross.

Wholeheartedly, I stand on my theory that if an opposite-sex friend has an issue with how you choose to set boundaries in your marriage or they choose not to respect those boundaries, they are not void of romantic feelings. From what I have witnessed from some other married couples who have had drama issues with opposite-sex friends, the "friend" either wanted one of them or both. Yikes.

Boss and I are not in a marriage with anyone else other than each other. The opinion of others regarding our boundaries is not our business. We do what works for us. And voilà! No drama. It's that simple.

I strongly believe that Boss and I no longer have issues with people attempting to cross boundaries in our relationship because we demonstrated respect for each other early in our marriage. When people see that you respect yourself, each other and what you have together you are more likely to be respected. That is a good thing because we love our relationships with friends and family, and we want to create many memories and pleasant experiences with them.

While we are establishing boundaries for others, we must also establish boundaries for ourselves and be mindful not to cross them.

The situation that taught us to create boundaries with ourselves was when we stepped outside of our own boundaries and vented about each other to a family member when both thought we could trust about a couple of disagreements we had with each other. After she instigated between the two of us some conflict stirred up.

We found ourselves having an argument that went like, "You told such and such xyz?" That was the last time that sentence came out of either of our mouths.

No one could cause problems in our marriage unless we allowed it. We decided that we would not allow it. There was no room for us to have our happy marriage interrupted by anyone, not even us. We decided then and there to discuss our issues with each other and not behind each other's backs. If I have an issue with my husband, he will be the first to know. There is also nothing I will say about him to anyone that I have not said to him.

One of the issues with venting to people outside of your relationship is that it isn't fair to triangulate them and put them in the middle of your stuff. This can be stressful and draining for others.

Sure, some people love to be in the middle of other people's issues, and they love to go back and forth between the two adding fuel to keep the fire burning. Those are the people you do not want to involve.

HERE'S WHERE I DRAW THE LINE

A firm boundary to set if you are in a relationship, is to disallow anyone to come between you and your mate and to check yourself when you are the ones causing the division between the two of you.

Boundaries in relationships sometimes might only involve the two of you. It wasn't a week after Tyrek had left for basic training before Boss posted his bed for sale on the Marketplace and turned his bedroom into his mancave. Normally, Boss is a procrastinator, which often gets up under my skin deeply. He must have had his vision for his mancave well thought out because he did not sit around on any of his ideas before he put his transformation plan into motion. We drove an hour to feel and see the gray interchangeable LoveSac furniture he settled on.

At first, I did not want to invade his space. I already had my own office space in the front of the house.

Boss wanted me in the mancave with him. When I went in there, he would ask me to stay. Or he would suggest we watch Television in there if the LoveSac was more comfortable for me.

Eventually, we spent more time in the mancave than we did in the gathering room. We set into a routine. Instead of settling on our big sectional in the gathering room, with my stack of books and word puzzles I went into the mancave and sat in my favorite place on the LoveSac each evening and on the weekend for weeks.

One weekend day, we were doing our usual chilling in the mancave. I left out to go to use the bathroom in our bedroom. After I walked out of my bedroom back into the gathering room, I noticed my stack of books and the magazine that held my word puzzle sitting on the ottoman.

I did not need a rocket scientist to break down for me that Boss had kicked me out of the mancave in a very passive way. My feelings were hurt. I walked into the mancave.

"You put my stuff out?"

"Yeah."

I stood there and looked at him, speechless. *Yeah? That was all he was going to say?*

My calm hurt feelings turned into a heat wave that flowed through my body. I could feel my body temperature dial quickly increasing. "You could have just said you needed your space instead of putting my stuff out when I walked away." I glared at him before turning around and going to join my stack of books and my word puzzle in the gathering room.

It did not take me long to return to his normal pleasant and peaceful wife. I completely understand his need for space. I was getting tired of being in there, but he was the first to break the redundant routine we had settled on every day in Tyrek's old bedroom. Still, I did not like being put out. When we discussed my eviction later that day, I expressed that I would have liked for him to better communicate with me instead of waiting for me to go to the bathroom, then put my stuff out of his room for me to collect on my way out the front door like I was a one-night stand who he never wanted to see again.

For several days after that, I would not spend time with him in the mancave when he wanted me to.

"Nah, you might put me out again." I sarcastically joked with him.

He laughed, pulling me close with a handful of my butt cheek.

The mancave was new to both of us. Boss wanted me there all the time. Eventually, he wanted me there some of the time. He was creating a boundary when he put my things out even though the way he chose to do it almost got his head cracked.

I'm joking.

Domestic violence is not cute. However, it might be okay to take a bat to an ironing board every now and then.

Most of the boundaries we set with each other in our marriage have fallen into place automatically, unspoken and understood. Some things need a deeper conversation. Like, on one family vacation when the boundary lines were blurry and after a disagreement that turned into a huge argument, we both needed to come to the table with a clearer perspective about what to never do again.

On one of our trips to New York, he lost his mind. He left me, and I literally got lost in New York—well, lost in Central Park but I felt like I was lost in the middle of the Big Apple with no one to turn to.

It all started because he wanted me to break the rules of the great Central Park by going the wrong way down a one-way road. I do not mind breaking the rules sometimes if breaking the rules will not get me stampeded over by horses and bicyclers.

The weather was perfect, and the scenery was beautiful as Boss, Cam, and I zipped around on rented scooters through Central Park on a warm July day. We were having the best time stopping to sightsee as we passed exhibits and taking pictures and videos of Bethesda Fountain and each other.

One of my goals was for us to get to the Cherry Hill Fountain. I thought for sure that fountain was where the *Friends* cast filmed for their opening credits but discovered months later that it is a look-a-like. However, we made it there, Boss snapped pictures and clips of me in front of it with my *I HEART NY* t-shirt on. We all wore New York t-shirts that day.

We were deep in the park when we realized our scooter rental time was ending, and it was time for us to head back to the front of the park, back across the street, and down in the subway to the rental location to return them.

Boss and Cam were on a scooter together riding ahead of me. I rode solo.

I was trying my best to dodge horses, their carriages, cyclists and stop at the red lights. Some of the cyclists were running red lights, nearly hitting pedestrians who were crossing the street.

After stopping at one red light, I could no longer see Boss and Cam ahead of me. When the light changed, I continued to ride in the one-way direction we were going in.

Boss passed me coming back my way in the opposite direction of the one-way. I did not know if he knew he was going the wrong way. He has a habit of going the wrong way down a one-way street. He has been making that mistake since we first started dating. I do not know how many times I have had to stop him from driving us down a one-way street in any given city.

As he passed, he waved at me to follow him.

"You're going the wrong way," I yelled at him, hoping he could hear me. I kept going, expecting him to turn around and come back the right way.

He came back and did the same thing. He made a U-turn and without stopping told me to follow him, and he kept going. Now, I was getting annoyed because he kept telling me to follow him down a one-way street the wrong way, and he was leaving me instead of listening to me tell him that I did not feel comfortable riding into oncoming traffic.

I continued along in the direction I was going—the right way. Unfortunately, the right way down the street was the wrong way to go to get out of the park. I stopped and asked a guy who was giving bicycle tours around the park. He gave me some directions that I thought I understood, but obviously I did not, or he gave me bad directions, one of the two. I am going to guess it was me because I have no sense of direction. Which made me even madder at Boss because he knew I lacked in the sense of direction department before he left me struggling in Central Park to find my own way.

My phone rang in my pocket with Boss' special ring tone. I made a mental note to change that to a breakup song later.

"Hello!" I had a straight-up attitude.

"Where are you?" He asked.

"I don't know. I can't believe you left me."

"We're waiting for you in the front."

HERE'S WHERE I DRAW THE LINE

I clicked the phone off without saying another word.

As I moved toward the directions I was given, I saw the tall familiar buildings that stood in the front of the park off at a distance.

I must be getting closer, I thought, and I perked up. I kept moving on my scooter. The buildings begin getting farther away. As the buildings moved backwards from where I was, I grew more anxious and angrier. I cursed the day that I went to this man classroom and asked for his number. Then, I cursed the day that I responded back to him when he found me on Myspace ten years later.

I pulled to the side of the street, dismounted the scooter, and looked for a way that I could legally go back in the opposite direction. I rolled my only friend—the scooter—toward a sign with the name of an exhibit on it. I entered. There was also a sign that forbids scooter riding beyond that sign. What I did not know is that I was entering some sort of forest.

Now, not only alone but also afraid, I traveled through the trail with my scooter in tow. It was almost as if the day had turned to dusk. It was dark in what seemed like the wilderness. I heard noises in the bushes all around me that sounded like animals. I was looking for yellow cat looking eyes to stare back at me. I saw no one in sight.

As I roamed hopeless and hopeful at the same time through this path, I felt all kinds of emotions. If Boss and I ever divorce, a flashback of this terror would be the reason.

Finally, I saw a young lady.

"Excuse me. Do you know the way out of here?" I asked her, searching her face for a speckle of empathy for the little lost black lady in the woods.

There was not one tiny spot of care in her eyes. She shook her head, no and kept moving. I figured at least I could keep up with her so I would not be alone. She quickly turned off the trail to go what seemed like deeper into the woods.

Alone again, I kept moving. *Ahhh!* I could see some hope ahead. It looked like a building I was coming up on. More people. I approached another lady.

"Excuse me. Do you know the way out of here?"

I silently prayed that she knew more than the last lady pretended not to know. She pointed me in the direction to get out. I was not too far from broad daylight again. I could see it in the short distance. I finally made my way out of there and back into civilization.

Boss was calling again. "Stay where you are, I'm coming."

I stood and waited for him. He obviously pulled up my location on Google maps. He and Cam came zipping my way.

"Come on." He instructed me to go the wrong way again.

"I am not going the wrong way. I do not feel comfortable going against all that traffic," I yelled at him and stood with my arms crossed.

After we stood on the side of the street going back and forth for about thirty seconds, I followed my husband, but I was not riding that scooter the wrong way in the middle of traffic. I pushed my scooter on the side since he insisted that we go that way, and I did not want to end up in the wilderness again. If he left me again, me and that scooter were going to catch a ride on a horse and carriage, and I would be arriving at the exit gate of Central Park like the queen he must have forgotten I am.

It took us ten minutes to get the scooters back to their owners. We were about an hour late. I was mad for another hour or two. I was still traumatized from roaming around in the wilderness alone and from the fact that Boss left me to fend for myself in Central Park in New York City in the beginning. Now how was he going to explain to Theresa and Bobby if an unknown animal with cat-like eyes would have eaten their baby girl or if I would have gotten kidnapped by Gargamel? His castle is out there in the park somewhere.

HERE'S WHERE I DRAW THE LINE

Me and Bae had to hash this one out one on one, face to face sitting across from each other at the hotel lobby's table. He apologized to me, and we established a boundary. Never let me get lost in New York alone EVER again.

The word *no* is a word that many people find difficult to say without feeling guilty. I used to be that person too. I thought I had to give an explanation with my no. People who have a hard time saying no tend to have a hard time holding firm to their boundaries as well.

Saying no doesn't always feel good and might feel uncomfortable sometimes. It's not always easy to stand on a necessary no or give a flat out no without apologizing or explaining yourself to make the no feel lighter on the receiver—or make you feel better about giving it.

I am a giving person. I say yes a lot. That is just my personality. However, there are still times that I need to be selfish, put myself first and say no. Since I know how important it is for me to do that, I also need to accept the same from others.

Boss spoils me real good, so good that when he says no to me, it feels like a blow to the chest. I will be all up in my feelings at first because I practice allowing myself to feel my emotions. Sometimes I can't believe he has the audacity to utter such a word as an answer for something I want him to do. It's rare, but it happens. Regardless of how I feel about that no, I must respect his right to say no.

While saying no to others is one thing, I had to also be able to say no to myself. It was crucial for my growth and physical, mental, and spiritual health to do so. The hardest boundaries to stick to have been the ones I have had to set for myself because that means seeing the err in my own ways.

I have to say no to myself in order to stay physically healthy. When I was diagnosed with high cholesterol, I had to create boundaries with myself around food and change the way I eat. I do not always stick to only healthy foods but for the most part I am mindful of what I eat, make sure I exercise and keep my doctor's appointments.

When my doctor gave me instructions on things to do to be healthy and manage the cholesterol issues, I had to establish boundaries with April.

The day I was diagnosed with high cholesterol I thought that meant I was about to die any day from heart disease. I was in my early thirties. I went into the doctor's office for my lab results. I sat in the room with the doctor as he called off everything else that was good then the one thing that was bad.

"Your cholesterol is elevated."

He told me what the numbers should be versus what they were. I sat quietly.

"You are still very young. I do not want to put you on medication now because that would mean you could be on the medication for the next fifty years."

I continued to sit quietly, listening, holding back tears, wondering why my father's genetics were attacking me now, at this age.

"Changes to your lifestyle may help to decrease your LDL—exercise and diet changes." He handed me a booklet outlining food that may decrease my cholesterol and foods to avoid.

As soon as I got in the car, I called my mom bawling.

"What's wrong?" my mom asked.

Between sobs I managed to tell her my devastating news, that was not as devastating as I thought.

"I-got-high-choles-tr-ol."

After talking to my mom and doing research, I realized I wasn't about to drop dead at any minute. I just needed to create boundaries for myself around the things I frequently put into my body. I have to say no to my fried chicken cravings 99.9 percent of the time.

To learn yourself, your needs and your own red flags is to know yourself so well that you can also say NO to yourself.

I have had to set several boundaries with myself. These are some of the things I had to tell myself in order to work toward becoming a healthier me that I will share with you:

—NO yourself enough to stop going into environments that harm you.

—NO yourself enough to stop occupying space with people who keep showing you that they don't mean you well.

—NO yourself enough to stop caring too much about what he, she and they say.

—NO yourself enough to stop allowing people to fill you up with their stuff when they are hell bent on continuing in the same mess and are making no efforts to change their situation.

—NO yourself enough to stop refusing to put weights down that you no longer have to carry.

—NO yourself enough to stop tolerating stuff that is breaking you down on the inside and making you feel less that who God called you to be.

—NO yourself enough to stop making things and people a priority that suck up all the space and energy you have to say yes to the things you need.

Say no to yourself when you are the one making the choice to allow things, people and situations to hurt you.

Saying yes when you need to be saying no is normally people pleasing behavior. Being brave does not always mean saying yes. Sometimes the brave thing to do is to say no so you can set yourself free.

Sometimes boundaries are crossed unintentionally. I have learned to examine the situation and have a conversation if I need to. Although I have gotten more experienced with boundary setting and maintaining them, I am not so quick to cut off people that I am close to for crossing a boundary, depending on that boundary. I know we are living in the time of the cut-off or cancel culture. These days, if someone makes a mistake, they are cut off in an instant without a chance to explain or redeem themselves. I don't operate that way.

Don't get me wrong. Not cutting someone completely off does not mean that I will not put space and distance between us if they fail to respect boundaries.

I have a sibling that I had to establish rigid boundaries with. He is blocked on everything he can possibly reach me on, he's not welcome in my home, I will not be around him but if by chance I see him, I do speak briefly and I keep moving.

None of these boundaries were set out of anger. They were set for peace of mind. I set boundaries with him faster than anyone else in my family did. A couple of my family members said that it was mean when I wouldn't allow him to come to my home during a holiday get-together. I am okay with not everyone agreeing with the boundaries I choose to set. Ironically, now none of them will allow him in their space.

As you know from my earlier chapter, "Blood is Thicker Than Water. So?" I am set free from feeling obligated to people just because they are related to me. My boundaries do not discriminate. Everybody can get one—or some.

One of my sons finally introduced us to a young lady he had been dating for a while. Although I want my boys to be in the best position possible and ready before they make children, I do want more grandchildren to spoil, so of course, I was excited to see him with a nice young lady who seems to have her head on straight.

I decided that even though I have the young lady's phone number, I would not open communication with her unless it was okay with my son.

He wasn't comfortable yet with us communicating too much. He thought that if we did, that would become too comfortable with calling me if she had issues with him, so I only contacted her when it was necessary, which was rare. I tend to shy away from my adult children relationship business unless they come to me to talk or for advice. I mostly wait until I am invited in.

I wanted to send KB a high school picture of himself standing on the track in his track uniform, but his phone was not working. I sent it to her and asked her to show it to him.

Hey! Yes, I'll send it to him. Is that at his track meet? LOL.

Yes. In high school. Lol I texted back.

The next day, he texted. *Ma, why are you sending pictures to people phone?*

I looked at the phone and thought, *Wait. Is he checking me?*

He was indeed checking me. He was reestablishing that silent boundary that we had—out loud. I smiled. I was proud that my son felt comfortable enough to set healthy boundaries with me.

I replied, *My apologies, I wanted you to see it.*

I guess I had gotten a little too comfortable for him.

Tyrek and KB always seem to be so secretive about their dating life. I have not been able to figure out why. Boss and I have always encouraged our children to talk to us about anyone they might like or be interested in. Even when they were younger, we normalized crushes. We did not attempt to force boundaries around their feelings toward liking girls.

Daneisha had no problem sharing stories about her love interests with me. I gladly listened. I did not see the point in freaking out when your young children like someone. Kids talk to opposite-sex friends face-to-face at school, so I didn't see the point in not allowing phone calls either, if the conversations are appropriate.

Liking boys was normalized for me when I was little. I did not run home and tell my mom about my first crush, the white boy named Michael Bray, in second grade. But she did not make me think I would be in trouble for liking boys.

By the time I got to fourth grade I called myself having a boyfriend or two. It was innocent of course. There was no kissing or no inappropriateness. The most touching I did with one of my boyfriends was braid his rat-tail on the back of his head.

While I was in elementary school, my mom had no problem with little Anthony coming to knock on the door for me to come outside and play. As I got older, she started to put boundaries in place when it came to boys. No boy other than my neighborhood friends, Brian and Dominic, was knocking on her door for me while I was in middle school. I am assuming it was because in elementary school a boy coming to play was viewed as innocent. Anthony was one of the two boyfriends I had in elementary school—until we broke up and he called me a black roach.

That is when me and my best friend, Tessa, agreed neither of us would *ever* go with him again. Looking back on elementary drama has always been hilarious to me.

When I was in middle school, my friends called on three-way if a boy was on the phone to ask for me just in case one of my parents answered the phone. There were no boys calling me directly until I got into high school. At fifteen years old, I was gifted a black pager from my sister and brother-in-law for Christmas and once I got a job, I got my own private line in my bedroom.

It is funny how our parents set boundaries for us, and we get older, we begin establishing our own boundaries for them to respect. Then, we have our own children, and the cycle repeats.

HERE'S WHERE I DRAW THE LINE

As parents, we may mean well but to maintain a strong relationship with our adult children, we need to respect their boundaries. Even in our attempt to help, we should be careful to set our own boundaries with our children and with ourselves when it comes to our children.

If we aren't careful, we can enable poor behaviors and hinder their growth by our actions.

I realized some time ago that I was suffocating my son's independence. When he was a teenager, I would complete all his paperwork. I applied for after-school jobs for him. I completed his college applications. When he had a question about something, I would just do what needed to be done for him instead of assisting him. Any research that he needed done, I was on it. I continued this behavior as he crossed the threshold into his twenties.

The co-dependency was not helpful for him in the long run. As he got older and I got tired, I got frustrated because he didn't complete things on his own. He wasn't following through with the important things. He was depending on me to do the things he should have been doing on his own and more efficiently by now.

When the light came on, I thought, *This is on me. I am projecting the frustration in the wrong place. It's me. I am the problem.*

I started pushing his responsibilities back his way when he tried to hand them to me. I also created a boundary with myself and decided not to voluntarily overstep. When I began seeing him enter his independence and handle his tasks on his own, I was proud of us both.

I learned a lesson through parenting each child. I was more seasoned by the time my next son began adulting. I always am here with guidance for all my children. I always will be, but the less hand on approach seems to be more freeing for me and in the long run, for them as well.

One of the reasons creating healthy boundaries between yourself and others is so important is if you do not, you might end up losing trust in people and yourself in general.

I have heard people say that they trust no one. Often, that kind of distrust comes from a lack of setting healthy and firm boundaries.

When we have poor boundaries or none, we open ourselves up to getting hurt more, getting taken advantage of, and allowing the wrong people in to occupy our space.

We might allow others to control parts of our life that should be personal decisions, make decisions that could be harmful to us and others, and we may even overstep into other people's spaces and lives frequently as well.

Attempting to change people or force them to change means that we are overstepping and often is intrusive. Trying to change people and succeeding in that rarely ever works out.

I had a friend that I thought needed me to save her. I had made my poor choices; I was in a better place and thinking more clearly. I had learned some lessons and matured some. I was carrying a li'l bag of wisdom, so why not help a friend? She lagged in the better choices department and kept repeating the same unhealthy behaviors. Because I had learned a thing or two about life and relationships and I cared about her so much I was supposed to save her from herself.

But I was not though. That was not my place.

Again, I lied to myself. My save-a-friend mode caused a lot of conflict in our friendship. I decided that she just didn't want to hear "the truth." Our honesty is aways the truth, right? It's not. Sometimes our suggestions are honest from our perspective, and we are indeed genuine when sharing that honesty, but it's still an opinion that may not always be that person's truth, even when it's ours. What we are saying might make sense and be sound and could also be helpful if received. It's just not our life to live. People can within their right, turn down loving advice and genuine gestures.

HERE'S WHERE I DRAW THE LINE

I want to genuinely see people happy. It doesn't matter if I know them or not but those that I love deeply I desperately want to see them happy and healed. That's okay that I want this for others. It's not okay to try to force it on them.

It is fine to want that for others, and it's okay to care. Kind people care about others and can empathize with their situations. However, it is not okay to go around on a mission to gather happiness for other people and try to set them free from their internal struggles. Those are the things they must do for themselves.

I could have been open to ways to support my friend without asserting myself into her decision-making process. Regardless of how much I thought she was making the wrong decisions or hurting herself, repeatedly.

I was on a path to healing. I was making better choices but that was the space I was in. My error was to also try to strong arm someone else to join me in that space when they obviously were not ready. I had the space to figure out life. Truthfully, I was still trying to figure out many aspects of my life. Though figuring out life looked different for me than it did for her, I had to accept that she didn't need me to save her. Nor did she want me to.

None of what I was doing to help was working for our friendship. I was always left feeling hurt, exhausted and worn out. She wasn't the one to blame. I was. I was trying to take on the responsibility of her life changes so that she can be happy.

My toxic codependent trait was rearing its ugly head. Thinking we are being helpful can really be hurtful. We can hurt others and ourselves by pushing against their personal boundaries. There are the people who do not want our help and then there are those who do. If we don't set boundaries around our own emotional well-being people will drain life out of us.

I am naturally a helper and empathic for the most part. I don't mind being the go-to person for some people some of the time, but I had to learn that I cannot be the go-to person for all people all the time. Outside of my clients, some days I receive text and phone calls from different people wanting to vent. That can be draining.

I had to make the decision to make boundaries with myself to protect my emotional well-being. One of the ways I do that is to no longer give space to people who are venting to me about the same thing repeatedly. If they are choosing the same situation and are not deciding to make changes to the things they can control, I do not allow them access to drain me.

I am learning to limit myself. I listen to my body and mindfully gauge my mood. If I am feeling mentally tired, I do not open my availability to others' problems. Boss reminds me often to relax, stop taking on everyone else's stuff, stop answering the phone, and take a break.

As I write this, it reminds me of an ironic and funny situation that happened recently. I had been having a hard time mentally, dealing with a loss and some other things that I was processing. On one day in particular, I was exhausted, but I had to adult briefly. I had been driving down the street for about 15 minutes when my car dinged. That ding let me know the car was sending me a message. I looked at the screen. The message across the screen read, *Consider taking a break.*

I had seen several smart safety features and warnings pop up but never this one. Not for the entire two years that I had been driving this car. I did not know exactly why the car indicated that I needed to take a break. When I came to my destination, I researched it. My car sends this message when the driver's attention level is low, and the driver seems fatigued.

The most ironic thing about that moment was that I did need a break. Not just a fifteen- or twenty-minute break. I needed to take some mental health days.

It is so important that we listen to what our body, mind, and spirit are telling us. Sometimes people will have to wait and so does everything else we have going on while we recharge and rebalance.

Setting boundaries is not a bad thing. Initially, it might be a bit of a struggle if you are not used to setting boundaries. I had to practice putting healthy boundaries into place until I felt comfortable setting guilt-free boundaries. With healthy boundary setting comes freedom.

Nine
Find Your Tribe

"Friends are like shoes—some loose, some tight, some fit just right. They help you as you walk through life. Thank you for being my size."
—Unknown

One of the best pieces of advice I ever saw online about friendship is a quote that says, "Find your tribe. Love them hard."

Not everyone is for you, and you are not for everyone. That's completely okay. That is something that took me years to accept. It was freeing to accept that not everyone has to like me. I don't encounter many people that I would say I do not like, even if they are not my cup of tea. To dislike someone because I don't like some of the things they do or some of their personality traits is not my style.

Friendships have come easy to me most of my life. I haven't had many hard friendships. Most of my friendships have been long and healthy.

I came to realize that God opens doors for the people to come into our lives who are a part of his plan he has for us.

FIND YOUR TRIBE

We don't have to force the door open to invite someone in that is naturally meant to be in our lives. Some may be there for a season, some for a lifetime. Even the season friendships can be good friendships.

One of my friendships caught me by surprise. I have known my Bestie Kisa for most of my life. We grew up in the same church, but we were never friends. We never tried to be. We were just cordial. I really didn't know if she liked me much at all because it didn't seem much like it. She was always looking at me with her nose turned up.

Kisa and I became friends after I took her a sentimental card to encourage her through a difficult time I had heard that she was experiencing. I asked a mutual friend to ask her if it was ok that I brought her something.

"I don't care," was the message they relayed back to me from her. I went and dropped the card off. We began to talk more personally. Through the conversations our friendship grew.

If anyone would have told either of us many years ago that we would become one of the closest people to each other, we both would have looked at them crazy because we wouldn't have been able to see the vision. This type of friendship we have was not in either of our plans, at least not with each other. Apparently, it was in God's plan. God knows who and what we need before we do and when we need it. Because of how we became friends I refer to her as my godsister, because she is my God-sent sister. She is the sister I was able to choose.

Our friendship reminds me of Pooh and Piglet. They have a friendship that is well-bonded and firm. Their quotes about friendship represent support, love, understanding, empathy, trust and compassion. To have a friendship that is a representation of all those things is special to me.

Her loyalty to me is unmatched. She and I have helped each other grow in so many ways. She is a sound voice for

me on many days but will be tens toes down when I need her to be.

Bestie Pooh, you were not that bad after all.

I used to think that I didn't want to make any new friends. That the friend circle I grew up with from middle and high school was enough for me, then I began meeting new people who were really cool, trustworthy, supportive, and genuine.

I met my friend Rineta at Arielle's. I would see her there almost every time I went to do open mic poetry or for other events. When I looked up, I saw her staring at me and smiling.

She is always smiling, I thought.

Her smiley, happy face did not match my normal unintentional resting furrow on my face. One night she offered me her Mary Kay card, so perhaps she was daydreaming about giving me a facial to rid my skin of the acne I might have had when she stared at me all those nights. Kind of like observation comes naturally for me, so I am assessing the behavior of random people around me, diagnosing them and formulating a treatment plan in my head.

Rineta and I clicked right away and immediately formed a close friendship. She is kind, loyal and will stop in the middle of anywhere and pray for me—or anyone.

I also met Rashad at Arielle's and now that he is married, I have gained another great friend, his wife, Danielle. Rashad was there through most of my dating shenanigans getting me right together with his honest and straightforward approach to our friendship.

God knew I was going to need my sister Ashlyn. We met through our daughters. She was the closest person I had to family outside of Boss and the Kids when I moved to Crestview. She was my biggest support when Boss was deployed to Afghanistan. Although neither of us looked for any reciprocal actions from the other, our friendship embodies reciprocity.

I met a few other wonderful, amazing women during our eight years living in Crestview who showed up for me in some way or another in ways that I will never forget. Whether it was through conversations, birthday celebrations, lunch dates, and much-needed girls nights they have all been a blessing to me.

I have several friends not mentioned by name, that I love dearly and that I consider very special to me. I mentioned these friends specifically because they are some of the friends I met in my adult life and formed close-knit relationships with. Most of my other closest friends I have known since I was a child or a teenager.

There is a belief among women that it is hard to form new close and trustworthy friendships with other women during adulthood. I do not call this belief a myth because for some people this may be true. I can understand the struggle for some people because I've met a couple who I could have left exactly where I first said hello. Trusting those around me is important to me because I love hard and genuinely. I do not want to be held back from trusting others because of a few people's inability to radiate genuine sisterhood. However, we do have to check ourselves and examine if we are the problem when several of our friendships are hard to maintain. In order to gain and keep genuine people around you, you must also be genuine.

God has been extremely good to me. He's blessed me to not only have friends who have been my family since I was very young, but also to have formed healthy and genuine relationships with people as an adult. I am also thankful for my mindset to pour into my friendships, build them up, keep them going, and foster growth. Having healthy and genuine relationships has helped me tremendously to sift away the one-sided or toxic ones.

One of my longest friendships is still closely knit to this day. It got rocky many times, but the good outweighs the bad.

Back in the good old days before we had responsibilities, Tip and I would sit in my room, write songs, sing, and listen to music. She was the singer. I was the writer. I already told you my mama said I can't hum a tune.

Like Kisa, Tip and I grew up in the same church as well. When we were teenagers, we decided that we were cousins. I guess we spoke it into existence because when Kelvin and I wed, she became my cousin through marriage.

For the short time she lived with us when we were in high school, I loved having her there. It was like sharing a room with a sister my age, plus my sisters had long moved out by then. I was able to spend so much more time with her while she was there because she wasn't allowed out of the house much. There would be days when her mom would allow her to walk to our house with enough time for her to make it to our door, us to exchange hellos and goodbyes, and she was back on her way home to meet her curfew.

Tip and I were walking down the street to the park on a weekday afternoon after school. We got to the end of my street, and her mom and dad pulled up as if alerts went off to let them know Tip's outside and where to find her.

"What you doing out here being grown?" her mother fussed.

"We are just walking to the park." Tip timidly answered her mother's question.

"Oh, you think you can do what you wanna do?" She made Tip turn around and go back to our house. Of course, I went back too. I was not going to the park alone. I was confused about what we were doing to be "grown."

Her stay at our house was cut short when two of her family members told her mom there was a boy in our house. There were always boys in our house. Tony had friends that came over and a couple of them were our mutual friends we grew up with. We were both sad when she had to leave our house and go live wherever her mother was staying

temporarily until their house was ready to move back in. We couldn't spend much time together because she wasn't given the same freedom, but we were still two peas in a pod. We made up for all that lost time when we became adults.

Most importantly, regardless of all the ebbs and flows, ups and downs, and bumps along the way of our friendship, she has shown up for me in a several big ways with no questions asked.

Unfortunately, length of time does not always keep friendships tight and bonded. Friendships, just like romantic relationships, take pouring into in order to keep them afloat. It takes two people who are both giving.

From my perspective, I don't have any long friendships with those I consider close to me that have failed or no longer exist. However, I have let some of my expectations go and have begun to view my place in some people's lives differently and vice versa.

If I am honest, I have a closer relationship with some of the friends that I have gained as an adult than I do with some of them that I formed as a teenager.

When I started feeling like I wasn't as important to some of my long-time friends, I began to distance myself. I tend to do that. After so long of feeling abandoned or less important to those who are important to me, I withdraw. Withdrawing was not the answer. I had to free myself from holding people to things that they were not obligated to do and learn to focus on those who genuinely and freely wanted to show up as the friend that I needed.

I learned to be okay with loving my friends exactly in the space we are in. Some friends who once were the closest to me, I may never regain that closeness again, but the love is there. They are great people. I cherish all our memories together and I always will.

There are a few women I've known most of my life who I may not be as close to them as I once were, but I love them, nonetheless. They may not be my first choice to call on in my time of need or in a time of happiness. I might not be their first choice either. That's completely okay.

In one of my friendships, I decided to close a revolving door. That doesn't mean that I cut off my friend. We are still very close. In fact, she's one of the closest of my friends that I love having in my life, and I wish to keep it that way. What I mean by closing the revolving door, is that I decided that the last fall out was the last one. Because we have been friends since we were kids, I took into consideration that we grew up together, so there would of course be ups and downs along the way. We learn a lot about ourselves and the people around us as we grow up and mature.

We had so many fallouts during our friendship that by the time we were thirty and still having fall outs, I decided that there would be no more. I am okay with disagreements. I am not okay with falling out a hundred times and someone not speaking to me for months. The fall outs were not about anything serious enough to stop speaking, in my opinion. As much as I love her, this is a boundary I set for myself and a freedom that I claimed.

I cannot control if she ever decides to fall out with me again, but if she does, I will no longer allow her access to the same closeness to my heart nor to take up so much space in my life again. Falling in and out and then having to rebuild what was lost is exhausting. The older I get the more I love peace of mind. When you genuinely love your friends, fall outs hurt. I was tired of hurting, so the door no longer revolves. It opens to go out of, but there is no longer a re-entry

point. Prayerfully, this friendship has grown beyond the fall-outs.

FIND YOUR TRIBE

We cannot hold people hostage in friendships that they no longer want to be in. I used to call to try and fix things I did not break and get ignored. I set myself free from that. I grew up and realized that others may not value friendship the same way at the same time. They may learn to value it later. I can value the people in my life without trying to fix everything all the time.

Many people have had to close the door on friendships that meant the world to them. If something is hurting, you repeatedly, you must decide if you want to keep that pain on repeat or set yourself free from it. Toxic friendships exist just like toxic romantic relationships exist. Neither are good for our mental health. That is not to say that it is easy.

Friendship is an intimate connection. Walking away from a friendship can hurt just as badly, if not even more, than a romantic breakup. We create unforgettable memories and share our deepest secrets with some of our friends. Some of them are there through our greatest moments and our toughest moments. It is safe to say that losing a best friend can feel like our entire world has been torn apart, all while they are still alive and well. All things that are necessary to do are not easy to do.

It is easier to point out imperfections in our friends than it is ourselves sometimes. I think one of the greatest and bravest things we can do as a friend is take accountability that we are not perfect friends either. I don't know about you, but I know I am not a perfect friend. Just in case you think you are, I will just go ahead and tell you that you are not.

Since I am aware that I am not, I have forgiven several times over and given the benefit of the doubt more times than I probably should have. We can allow room for our friends to make mistakes while remembering that mistakes are not intentions to harm, and neither are mistakes repeated. Then they become a habit and intentional.

The best way for me to decide if a friend is worth holding on to is to pay attention to their genuineness. If I see anything phony or fake in their approach to our friendship, then I know that is not a true friend. If they are purposely doing things to hurt me, then I know that is not true friend behavior. I only want to be surrounded by people whose goal is to love, encourage, uplift, support and be free. Just the same as I have identified what type of close friendships I want, I need to also be the same kind of friend I desire.

I like to reflect on my friendships. It keeps me grateful. I love the connection I have with the amazing friends in my life. Every memory is worth having and worth holding on to. It is a blessing when you can get comfortable and settle into those compatible friendships. Because I tend to go hard for my tight friendships, I cannot afford to have people around me who seem to only take without replenishing.

There are many great people in the world, but being a great person doesn't make me compatible with everyone. I accept that. One thing that I am grateful for is that I have not had to decide to cut off and block anyone I considered a friend nor have had to decide to never speak to them ever again.

Don't get me wrong, I have moved some people around on my priority list. I have had to release hurt feelings. You can't be free if you're holding on to negative emotions day in and day out.

I understand that some people have had to completely cut some friends off for a good reason. I'm not going to pretend some people don't purposely do things to harm their friends.

If you are one of those people and you have not healed yet from being hurt by someone you once trusted, take the steps to release that hurt. This does not mean allowing them

FIND YOUR TRIBE

back into your life. Releasing it means that you are setting yourself free. You deserve freedom.

I am grateful that I found my tribe. There's a popular saying that advises us to keep our circle small. I say, keep your circle genuine, as in with genuine love and respect. It doesn't matter if your circle holds five or fifty friends, just keep it genuine.

Life is too short not to spend it enjoying healthy friendships. We need to be set free to be our authentic selves in our friendships. If you haven't already, I hope that you also find your tribe and love them hard.

Ten
Who Dat Woman? (Or Man)

"I was once afraid of people saying,
'Who does she think she is?' Now, I
have the courage to stand and say,
"This is who I am."
 —Oprah Winfrey

Beliefs about who we are start in childhood. Finding out who we are or becoming who we are destined to be happens later in life for some people. A lot of people know who they were told they are and who they were told they are supposed to be.

I had several nick-names when I was younger and throughout my life. Different people called me whatever they decided based on what stood out to them about me. As I mentioned earlier, one of my aunts called me Chicken Legs and Sticks because I was skinny. To this day, one uncle calls me Gidget because I was small for my age and another uncle had been calling me Showers or April Showers ever since I was a small child into adulthood, until he passed on. A member of the church called me Pretty Hair, I am assuming because my hair was well-kept and well, pretty.

One of my sisters called me Whoop because I would do the whoop dance for her and her friends at their gatherings as they cheered me on. A friend of mine that I met while working at Chase, called me Whoadie which led to my sister then calling me Whoadie. My brother Chris calls me Ink Spot. There is some colorism attached to that but I love my skin complexion, so that doesn't bother me.

When Boss and I was dating he called me Brownie. My last name was Brown at the time. Jokingly, my friend Jameelah adds all my previous last names and my current last name after my first from time to time. She'll address me as April Lewis Brown Jones.

All these names apply to me in some seasons of my life but none of them are names I made up for myself. They were all made up by others to define me in some kind of way. None of these nicknames were bothersome for me other than the Chicken Legs and Sticks.

Other than nicknames, people have defined me by their perception and called me other things that were both pleasant and not so pleasant. That's just a part of life that I don't think any of us are exempt from.

If we are not careful, we can allow how others define us to destroy our self-worth and interfere with how we define ourselves. The negative perceptions and beliefs we think about ourselves and who we are can obstruct our paths and purpose.

Let my mother tell it, I always moved to the beat of my own drum. I agree with her that I've always been my own person for the most part. She had her own plans for me when I was a child. She wanted to teach me the things she loved to do. She bought me a sewing machine that sat on the closet shelf because I would rather be outside playing football in the street with my brothers, climbing trees or playing card games, board games (Battleship in particular), and zooming hot wheels around on the floor with my brother Chris, and apparently getting launched off seesaws.

My mother crochets beautiful blankets, clothes and accessories. She attempted to teach me to crochet. It wasn't that I couldn't learn. I can crochet a circle if not anything else. I wasn't focused enough to become as great as she is because I wasn't all that interested.

Once I was given daughters, I started to understand the desire my mother had for me to show interest in some of the things she loved. That's the point of having a daughter, right? But it doesn't work like that.

Kiaria spent a lot of time with me when she was growing up, but we didn't make as many mother-daughter memories as I would have liked when she was a teenager. I didn't get to help her mother shop for her prom dress or see her leave for the prom. By the time Kiaria graduated high school and went into the military, I had already gotten remarried and left Jacksonville.

Daneisha is a lot younger than her, and because she lived in the home with me full-time from age teen to seventeen, I had a lot more time and experiences with her. I did get to take her to shop for a prom dress, snap several pictures and see her off. I had a more hands-on role in raising Daneisha. I wanted Daneisha to wear her hair the way I liked it and dress the way I liked her to dress. That was all good until she began to grow into her own styles that fit her personality. So, I went from putting crinkles in her hair to sewing hair in her head, at her request. She didn't want the box braids I wanted her to wear, but when she decided to let her relaxer grow out and wear her natural hair, I was ecstatic. When she got old enough to wear makeup, I still couldn't fulfill my desire to make certain that she had a fancy makeup drawer organizer filled with eye shadows and lip sticks because she didn't like

WHO DAT WOMAN? (OR MAN)

anything more than lip gloss. That just wasn't her style. That was mine.

I never sensed that my mother took my lack of interest in her interests personally. As I grew as a bonus mother raising a girl, I discovered that Daneisha rejecting my ideas and wants for her own, were not personal. She had to have room to grow into her personality and her independent ideas.

Allowing our children to have their own minds is what teaches them to think for themselves, to learn who they are, and evolve.

KB is my athlete. He has played football, run track and now he is a boxer. I was skeptical about the football because of the injuries, but he really wanted to play. Boxing is harder for me to become comfortable with. He is tall, so I would rather him have built his basketball skills and dedicated himself to that or continued in track.

He cracks me up when anyone calls him another boxer's name. I don't care if they refer to him as Mike Tyson, he replies, "I'm me." He could just take the compliment and go with it. Instead, that is his way of creating his own identity incomparable to anyone else—even though he looks up to the legends and aspires to be just as good or better.

A lot like me once he wants something, KB has always been the type of person to go hard after it. He is great at what he does. Still, if I could choose a different path for him, I would. Even though uneasy about his career choice, I will genuinely always support him. My fears or desires should have nothing to do with him meeting his goals, succeeding in his dreams, and becoming who he is purposed to be. That is my cross to bear and my problem to solve.

I love his determination. That same determination has gotten him into trouble though. When he was on restriction from games, Boss would place the game controllers in our room. We knew KB was sneaking the controllers. Boss decided to set up his laptop on a table in our bedroom to record. I do not know how KB knew the laptop was recording. Maybe he overheard us talking.

After a day of recording, Boss chuckled while looking at one of the videos. "Come look at this."

I looked at the video play back on the laptop. The footage showed our bedroom door slowly opening. We could see KB's white t-shirt just above the bed as he crawled on the floor toward the laptop. We watched him cover the laptop up with a towel right before the video went black.

The entire video and his audacity were all quite amusing, but the most amusing part was when he uncovered the laptop and crawled back toward the bedroom door after he had accomplished his mission to confiscate the game controller.

Boss and I laughed long and hard.

Tyrek moves freely.

When he was in elementary school, I took him to the doctor for a well check. They gave him a cup to collect a urine sample. He went into the restroom and when he was finished, he placed the urine cup into the sample collection window.

The nurse came into the room where we waited for the doctor.

"We need another sample. This is water," she said.

I laughed myself to tears.

"Tyrek, you can't put water in the urine cup. It must be urine." I told him between giggles.

"I didn't have to pee." He responded with a straight face.

That was such a Tyrek thing to do. It was best to just let Tyrek be Tyrek. There was no other way around it.

Camden is not quite a teen yet but still shocks me nearly every day with some new inappropriate information he learned at school that is way above what he should have obtained in his knowledge bank at his tender age.

I am not mad at his comfort level with me and his dad though. He is an open kid. I would never have asked my parents some of the things Camden has asked us, especially at ten years old.

WHO DAT WOMAN? (OR MAN)

I was driving him home after I picked him up from school one day. "Mom when can I say the D and the H word?"

"Why do you want to say those words? Do your friends say them?"

"Yes."

"You can say darn." I compromised.

"That's not as fun," he said, arguing for his permission to use swear words.

"When you become an adult, you can say whatever you want if it feels good saying it and you do not feel bad about it," I told him.

"What about the A word?"

I laughed. At that point I was done with the conversation.

We have also been open with Camden on an age-appropriate level when he is curious or when teaching him things. He might have made up his own, but we didn't make up nicknames for body parts or sugar-coated anything that should be taught factually to him. When Cam was much younger, while we were teaching him about appropriate and inappropriate touching, we taught him that his male part is a penis and not a wee-wee or ding-dong.

I was told that it was inappropriate for a parent to teach their small child the real words. I do not think that it is. It teaches more comfortability with your own body. The nice thing about being set free is not allowing anyone to dictate to you about who you are as a parent. I would rather teach him right at home instead of letting him learn wrong from the world.

I certainly guided my children but learning to enjoy who they are without driving myself crazy trying to change them is freeing.

Not only do you have to set yourself free from other people's wishes about who they would prefer you to be or what they envision for your life, it is healthy if you also set yourself free from being the one who tries to control what you want someone else to be.

Accepting people for who they are does not mean that you have to agree with them. For instance, my parents may not agree with some of my parenting techniques and vice versa. I may not agree with my children's parenting techniques and vice versa. Some of their choices in their life may be things we may have to agree to disagree about, but respect is not trying to change who they are. Just the same as I don't want anyone to try to change who I am.

Not all things that we disagree with about other people's choices are harmful to them. Someday our views may change as we change. We may begin to see and understand people in a different light.

I do understand when someone is making choices that are harmful to themselves and others, it is a harder situation. Actions might have to be taken to help them to create a healthier path. That's a different story. Even then, sometimes we are left with no choice but to step back, pray and let it be.

My Aunt Juanita was one of the sweetest women I knew. She is my father's oldest sister and one of my favorite aunts. She taught me piano lessons until I decided that I no longer wanted to miss going to Qunicy's or Ryan's after church on Sundays. I enjoyed spending that time with her.

Not long after my Aunt Nita passed away, I had a dream about her that encouraged my final choice for a difficult decision. I was working in a group practice about thirty minutes away from the home we lived in at the time. Boss was preparing to deploy to Afghanistan. I was scared, anxious, and unprepared because is anyone really prepared for their loved one to deploy to a war zone? I was on an emotional rollercoaster.

KB was in college, Daneisha would be leaving for the military soon, and it would be me, Tyrek, and Camden. I pondered over the best flexible working option for me and my family. I played with the idea of stepping out on faith and renting an office independently for the first time. This meant I would be relying on the one directory I was listed on to gain referrals. Mostly all my clientele came through the group practice where I was renting an office. This would not be a source of clients for me any longer if I made this decision.

Before Boss' deployment came up, the owner, whom I rented the office gave me insight on some of the changes she would be making and asked if I would be staying amid the changes. At the time of that conversation, my plans were to stay. She was making changes to the contract based on her expenses. This meant that she was going to start charging more money, which I didn't have a huge problem with.

Now, since Boss was deploying, I felt that the best decision for our family was for me to be closer to home and closer to Cam's school. He was starting kindergarten.

I decided to reach out to a lady about an office near home. Her price was right. The pros were, I would not be paying as much as I would be if I stayed in the group practice and I would be twenty minutes closer to home; the cons were, I wouldn't have a receptionist or a biller for my claims, and the clients were no longer guaranteed. This was a scary decision to make.

I sat down with the owner of the group practice to let her know about my decision to leave in 6 weeks. She was not happy about my choice. Some of the things said in our conversation left doubt in my spirit. One of the reasons being because I respected her. I valued our professional relationship, but I cared about her on a personal level, and she helped me a lot during my licensure process.

Also, some of the things she said left me feeling like she had a sense of entitlement for me to stay. I left the conversation with internal conflict, questioning my decision, which I thought I was so sure about.

After praying about it, I had the dream about my aunt. In the dream I was sitting down next to her. The words she spoke to me that stood out the most were, "You are worth more than you know."

I needed to believe in myself. If you don't believe in yourself, no one else will. I decided that I was going to rent that office closer to home and go into private practice completely on my own. The clients were going to come because I am good at what I do. I was under no obligation to anyone. I owed it to myself to do what was best for me and my family. I would define my own path because I was free to do so, and I did.

Since day one, I have not had any struggles getting clients. Even when I moved to Central Florida after Boss retired, all things fell in place and doors opened freely.

Now every time I doubt myself, I am reminded of my aunt's words to me, and that God has a purpose for me and there is not one thing that He purposed for me to do that will fail. I tell those doubts to set me free.

All it took was for me to believe in whose I am, who I am and what I can do. We need to own who we are. Until we stop disowning some of the parts of who we are, we will not reach our best self and we may allow where others think we should be to hold us back from receiving more.

I have always been a go-getter. I got my first job when I turned sixteen. It was two weeks before my sixteenth birthday when I walked into the $7 Clothing Store and asked for a job application. The supervisor told me that I had to be sixteen to apply. I counted down the days until my birthday. The first thing I wanted to do was go back and apply for that job.

WHO DAT WOMAN? (OR MAN)

My mother took me back on the first Saturday after my birthday. I filled out the application and turned it in. I called every couple of days to check on the status of my application until the supervisor told me to come in for an interview.

I spent my work hours unboxing clothing, taking the plastic wrapping from them, putting them on hangers and hanging them on retail racks and cashing out customers on the register. I loved that job mainly because I was able to buy things for myself and get my own phone line in my bedroom.

Once I started making my own money, I slowly squeezed pants into my wardrobe.

"You think you're slick," my mom said with contempt, one eyebrow raised. We stood in the junior's section of JCPenney's. I had a pair of size zero blue jean wide leg pants in my hands.

"These are like gauchos."

I'm sure she didn't agree with my rebuttal nor moved by the convincing look I gave here but she didn't make me put them back either.

My second job at McDonald's was a lot more fun to work at. There were other teenagers working with me. My manager was a loud, no-nonsense lady, but she was mostly kind.

There was a spring break event going on at Jacksonville Beach on a Saturday that I was scheduled to work. My shift started that morning, and I wouldn't get off until midafternoon. All my friends were going, and I wanted to go so badly. One of my friends would be driving her mom's car.

I did not want to call in, so I concocted a plan to get out of work the next day. Kelvin had a death in his family. The Friday night before the spring break event I went to work and told my manager that I had a death in the family and needed to get off early on tomorrow for a funeral that I had no intention on attending. She told me she would get back to me. I moped around my entire shift that evening as if I was so sad. She did not get back to me before my shift was over.

My mom picked me up after my shift ended. "Did you tell your manager that you had a death in the family?" My mom asked me after I got in the car.

I am sure if I was of a lighter skin complexion my face would have been beet red. Here I was moping around McDonald's for my entire shift and unbeknownst to me, my manager had called my mom and asked her if we had a death in the family. My mom obviously told her no. I was embarrassed just thinking about how I pouted around, with my eyes lowered and my head hung during my shift while she knew I was pretending. She could have told me she had talked to my mom. Ms. Chris is wrong for that.

I went to work the next day. I took a change of clothing with me. My friends picked me up from work when my shift was over, and we headed to the beach.

I do not know if I quit McDonald's or if I got fired. I wore my work shoes to my sister's house when I went over to spend the night. She took me home so my mom could drop me off to work. It wasn't until I got home that I realized I left my only pair of non-slip shoes at my sister's house. I called to let my manager know I wasn't going to be in that day and why.

"If you don't come to work, you can bring in your uniform," her loud intimidating voice bellowed.

I took my uniform. Maybe she didn't believe me because of the one time I lied about the death in my family and faked sad the entire shift. That was enough to break trust, but she could have just asked my mom—again.

I moved on to the next job. I was seventeen and enjoyed having my own money, so I wouldn't let that one job hold me back from making it. I was in Business Cooperative Education in school. I had an interview set up through that class at Prudential Insurance Company. Some other classmates and I interviewed for the position. I went into that interview wearing a flowered satin-like black dress with short heels. I pushed the nervous flutters that arose from my stomach back down my throat and remained confident as I interviewed for an entry-level position. If I got the job, I would be posting incoming insurance payments to customers accounts. I did get the job.

I only had four classes my senior year. I left school at 10:04 a.m. every day and went to work in the office at Prudential from one to five p.m. I rode the city bus to work. My mom barely drove her car, so I begged my dad with teary eyes to let me drive my mom's car.

"You would have to be on the insurance to drive that car."

"I will pay it." I promised him.

He gave me the keys, and I was gas happy! I was all over Jacksonville in that little corolla.

After the job at Prudential, I worked office jobs in mortgage, banking, procurement, or medical insurance positions for most of my adult life. There were a few random data entry jobs sprinkled in between.

I am a go-getter—and I am not a quitter—but I changed my entire career plan after one bad day of substitute teaching.

I changed my major from human services to education. Briefly. I took the General Knowledge Teaching examination and passed it. I thought I wanted to be a teacher at that time. I soon found out that dealing with other people's children in real life was nothing like teaching my stuffed animals and dolls when I was little girl. The stuffed animals and dolls listened well. Those little Kindergartens I substituted for did not.

After the two little kindergarteners teamed up to make sure my brief stay in their teacher's place was nothing short of miserable and stressful, I opted completely out of the idea of teaching altogether and went back to my God-given calling. So yeah, if I can say I quit anything. I quit that idea real fast.

I am grateful that I did follow my heart and my passion. I have thrived in my career as a therapist. Once I realized that I was gifted to work in the field, I went after it with all my heart. As a child, I would switch back and forth between wanting to be a teacher or a child psychologist when I grew up.

I decided on psychology by the time I began college. After I received my associate in arts degree, I realized there was nothing I could do with an AA degree, so I got my bachelors in arts degree. Then, I realized that there was nothing I wanted to do that I didn't need a master's degree to do. I went back to school without taking a break in between and I completed my master's degree program.

After I completed my BA degree, I was told that I should take a break. I was working full-time; I had two children, and all of that combined was a lot. I refused to listen to that. I think the person who gave me that advice meant well, but to keep going until I meet my goal is an element of who I am.

After completing my master's degree, I searched for jobs in my field. Every position that I was interested in required a license.

Well then, I guess I'll be getting licensed as a marriage and family therapist, I decided.

The way the door opened for me was so seamless that I knew it was God. I was talking to one of the veterans who worked in the Jobs Plus center with me. I told her of my plans to start working on my licensure. I had no idea that she was able to help me in any way. I would stop and have random conversations with her on several occasions. She provided me with the contact information for a lady who owned a mental health agency.

Whoever said that people could be mentioning your names in rooms you have never stepped foot in was not lying. Whoever says keep your plans to yourself and move in silence is not always right.

When I contacted the woman at the agency, she told me that she had heard a lot about me from a lady whose name I did not recognize, and that I come highly recommended. That was the start of my career as a Marriage and Family

WHO DAT WOMAN? (OR MAN)

Therapist, Intern. I walked right into a paid internship as a contracted therapist with no hassle.

The way that door opened for me wide and without force blew my mind. I was used to working face-to-face with clients since I was leaving a career counseling position. The press was that I had to go into people's homes and the tons of paperwork felt insurmountable. The major difference was that this type of counseling was on a whole other level with tons of layers.

I was a go-getter though. I was going to learn everything I could. I regularly attended seminars, supervision meetings with my state qualified supervisor, watched videos that were suggested by other therapists, and I read, read and read. If I could have opened my head and poured in all the knowledge I could get my hands on, I would have.

I still am a knowledge leech. I have a habit of reading five or more books at a time and purchasing more courses than I can take in a small time, but I always get through them, eventually.

Since I seek to be in the know about most things in my field, I have had to remind myself on several occasions that it is impossible to know everything. One of the hardest things that I have had to do during my career is to settle on a niche. I want to do so much that I can't settle on just one. However, there are certain areas that I am much more knowledgeable in than others.

As a therapist, I must be able to say, "This is out of my scope of practice."

I am okay with that now, but at first, I did not want anything to be outside of my scope of practice. I wanted to be great at everything that came my way. That might sound good and all, but trying to be great at everything can be one of our biggest downfalls. It is accepting that although we can be great at many things at once, we do not need to be great at everything in order to be effective.

Having too much on our plates can be a stumbling block as well.

When I was trying to do too much at once, I had to accept that something had to go on the waiting list.

Sometimes it is a matter of prioritizing, which might mean placing something on hold when there is too much on your plate. Earlier, I mentioned that someone gave me some advice to take a break in between my bachelor's and master's degree. That was something I chose not to do; I am glad I didn't. But there were times in my life that I did have to choose to put some things on the back burner in order to grow in other areas.

Being a go-getter works for achieving my goals, fulfilling my purpose and succeeding. It also means that I need to have balance so that I do not burn out. When burn out has set in, the things I enjoy doing may no longer be enjoyable and it has taken me longer to reach some goals.

Setting myself free from burn out as a go-getter might look like taking less clients while I work on a book. It might look like purchasing self-paced courses for further education instead of those that require my immediate time. It may look like listening to some audio books while driving or cleaning when I do not have time to pick up a book.

One of the things I am grateful for is to have a husband that is patient and understanding enough to allow me the space and time I need to accomplish goals. Not stressing about keeping the home running and following my dreams is one reason I rarely experience burn out. Boss is truly my partner and a team player.

In all my discovering of who I am—whether it be all the things that tied me to my nicknames, my career titles, a go-getter, a mother, a wife or any of those things—I have always reminded myself that I am God's child. Before anything else, the very essence of my existence is in Him.

Eleven
Eh? So You Thought?

"Sometimes we create our own
heartbreak through expectations."
—Unknown

When my ex and I broke up, I took care of KB and Tyrek on my own until Boss and I married. I kept a consistent job. Sometimes I did overtime when it was available. I made sure they had health insurance. I maintained the bills that kept a roof over our head and comfort. I provided all their needs and some of their wants. They were in private school. I had a scholarship that did not pay for the entire year's tuition, so the remaining balance was broken up as a monthly payment for the school year. I paid for that.

I would ask their father for money to help. He would never say no—either he did not answer at all, or he said yes and did not follow through. I would feel enraged. Rightfully so. I didn't make our children on my own. What I got the angriest about was the times he answered the phone, said yes, and then stood me up.

Once, he told me to meet him at a gas station across town from where I lived. I didn't have much gas, and I was on a strict budget, but if he was going to give me money, it would be fine for me to ride over there and get it.

When I got there, he wasn't there. I called him multiple times, and he didn't answer. I waited for about thirty minutes before I left and headed back home, clenched jawed and hot with fury. Not only did he have me drive over there, but he stood me up—big waste of gas and time.

After several times asking him for money that he said he would give me, but I never got, that little flickering light of reality finally beamed brightly into my mind.

I was getting mad and upset repeatedly about the same thing. I was doing this to myself. He wasn't doing this. I was. I already knew he made a habit of lying. That was one reason that we weren't together anymore. It was nothing new that he didn't provide for his children, so with all that in mind, what was I doing to myself? I was setting myself up every time I expected anything different. I had to find peace with the fact that he was not going to provide for his children in any way. My children are adults, and he still owes me over fifty thousand dollars in arrears from failure to pay over the years.

Expectations will have us messed all the way up. There are so many pieces and layers to its meaning when it comes to our perceptions. Having expectations is a form of holding on to hope. We believe that we deserve something from someone. It can be material things, behaviors, or thoughtfulness.

Our children did deserve better from him, but it was not conducive to hold on to that expectation when he had already shown time and time again that he had no intention of taking care of them.

We can have a false idea of our position in someone's life and how they see us or feel about us. I have been guilty of placing myself as a priority in some people's lives. Imagine that. Thinking that you were on someone's priority list, but they never made you priority—you did. You decided the level of importance you were in their lives based on a title, and now you have created these expectations that don't line up with their actions.

When I wrote my first book, I was so excited! This was big. The biggest thing that I thought I had ever done in my life, besides when I accepted Christ and bore children. I knew all the friends that I had been friends with for most of my life, those who I had become close to as an adult, my big family, everybody I knew who also knew me was going to be ecstatic.

They were going to clap for me so loud, long, and hard. They would congratulate me because they are so proud of what I've done. They were going to share the good news with everyone they knew. Certainly, they all would have a copy of my book sitting on their bookshelf or wherever they keep their collection of books. Not only would they have one for themselves; perhaps, they would gift some to others.

These were all the expectations that I had. When many of the people I thought would didn't follow through with these expectations, I felt let down. I was disillusioned.

After some time of sitting with my thoughts, pondering on my feelings, and talking to my therapist about friendships and family, I decided that I had let myself down. I placed expectations on people that I never should have.

I am still a firm believer in supporting your friends and family in ways that you can and if you can. These things tend to come naturally from those who are genuinely happy for you. If it does not, then I have learned to reconsider my place on their priority list, being mindful about who placed me there. Was it me or them? And how close do they consider themselves to be to me. Perhaps, not as close as I believed.

The first time one of my close friends since middle school had acknowledged that I was an author was after I wrote my fourth book. The first book I had released three years prior, and she had not once acknowledged it. I was close friends with several other women and they were hyping me up, showing excitement for my accomplishments, sharing my social media post about my books, giving me words of encouragement and all the other things I expected from close friends.

Now my fourth book had gotten her attention. She had questions for me about a book she was writing and at that point had decided to purchase my latest book. I gave her some websites to get information and answers to some of her questions. I did not mind sharing those resources.

It was when she asked if I could walk her through some of the things that I became annoyed. She did offer to pay me, but I wasn't interested in her money. I thought, *She's been calling me her best friend for over twenty years and the first time she acknowledges one of my greatest accomplishments was when she has questions?*

When we had a conversation about how I felt, five things in that conversation stood out to me.

When she said, "Just because I didn't say congratulations doesn't mean I wasn't proud of you."

"You've always been more sensitive than me."

"You didn't ask for support."

She reminded me of how she showed up for me when we were seventeen years old for some drama that went down with my ex.

Lastly, she took no accountability.

Those things opened my eyes even more. After thinking long and hard about the situation, I begin to take accountability myself. I took accountability for expecting anything more. For years prior to this, her behavior had not been what I consider best friend behavior. The emotional intelligence shows up when you realize that is not always a bad thing. People grow apart. My expectations should have changed along with the change in the dynamics of our friendship. Although I still consider her a friend and I love her just the same as I always have, there is no denying that we just weren't as close and hadn't been for a very long time. We live and we learn. We grow and we change.

If I was quick to cut people off, there are many times I would have cut off friends and family according to my own expectations. Instead, I removed myself from the priority list I had placed myself on and changed my expectations.

My disappointments were all about me and my perception. I have learned not to view all my relationships as equal. Some friendships are closer knit than others, just as some relationships with family. Our relationships with people may serve different purposes. When we learn what relationships serve which purpose then we can allow our expectations to fall in place accordingly.

I am not going to say don't expect anything from anyone or act like as humans we should not have expectations at all. We should. Nobody wants just one-sided or purposeless relationships with lovers, friends and family. I don't expect anyone I trust to do vindictive things to me. I expect them to be loyal enough to have the best intentions toward my well-being. I expect my husband to be faithful and honor our vows and the promises he made to me. I expect my children to respect me.

In my tribe of close-knit friends, we have defined what support for each other looks like. I expect love, support and honesty from those I consider my tribe.

I would love to have perfected this expectations thing, but I have not. However, I have learned, if my expectations are not clearly defined or I am placing expectations on people who do not want any parts of it then I am setting myself up to be hurt. On the flip side of that, I have had to set myself free from other people's expectations of me as well.

Twelve
Hey, Me! Get Out of My Way!

"It's not the load that breaks you
down, it's the way you carry it."
—Lena Horne

We talk about people getting on our nerves and so forth and so on, but have you ever gotten on your own nerves? I know I do. Sometimes I'm like, Oh *my goodness, Sis. Chilllllll.*

It's the overthinking that causes me to have to check myself. When I don't check myself, trust and believe, I have a friend that will certainly tell me to shut it off quickly. When it comes to work and some personal things, my business bestie, colleague and friend Stephanie will bring me back to earth when necessary. I love her straight to the point, no nonsense, get it together April with a twist of compassion and grace approach. We need people around us who rub off on us in a positive way. Just by example alone, she's helped me.

HEY ME! GET OUT OF MY WAY!

As far as typical everyday things, my mind is extremely creative when it comes to playing out a daydream that will have the very worst ending. Sometimes when overthinking, I develop the most bizarre situations and scenarios. I will sit and run an entire story in my mind based off a small piece of information.

There is a phrase inspired by a bible scripture that says an idle mind is the devil's workshop. My overthinking has given meaning to this truth. When I sit still and think, either I am going to create some master ideas in my head, my imagination is going to run away with me and it might not be a bad thing, or it is going to be a bad thing. Not all things that come to my mind when I am idling are horrible—still bizarre and weird maybe, but not always bad.

I planned a meditation session at my house for a few of my friends. I had a professional instructor come in to lead us in the session. We put down our palettes, blankets and wedges in my gathering room. Side by side, she had us stretch out on the floor and try to clear our minds. It's normal that during meditation, thoughts will come, but letting them pass is a part of the process. Letting them pass was my struggle.

It was completely quiet in the room, other than the instructor gently prompting us throughout. "Imagine the clouds in sky," she softly spoke, dragging her words.

I imagined the clouds in the sky, but my mind went into goofball mode. I lay there beside my friends thinking of funny what ifs—*What if this happened while we are laying here* or *What if that happened while we are laying here?* I didn't want to disturb the others, so I held my laughter best I could with tears streaming down my face. I thought about getting up and leaving the room so I could let the laughter have its way, but I stayed on my pallet and pleaded with my silly mind to focus on the imagery work as I was being prompted.

The instructor continued engaging us in the meditation gently and softly. I heard sniffing coming from both my friends. *Are they laughing too?* I looked over and they were both engaged in meditation. They had tears, too but it wasn't because they were laughing. I felt even more goofy. Here they were fully engaged and absorbing the healing that is coming from this experience, and all I can do is think of silliness. That made me want to split my side from laughter even more, but still, I held my giggles.

I can't wait to do another peaceful meditation session with my tribe. We all felt lighter coming out of the hour-long practice session. I most certainly did. Laughter is good medicine.

Overthinking has had me extremely anxious in the past about Boss going out fishing on a boat without me. As if I'm his protector. In a way, I am, but if we were out on a boat and things got rough out there, he would be the one trying to protect me.

When he'd say he was going out there in the ocean on a boat to fish, I started noticing a cycle. I wouldn't say I didn't want him to go because I did want him to get out and do what he loves to do. He didn't go that often. He deserved to do more of what brings him peace and joy. I noticed the closer it got for him to leave, I would get agitated and snappy.

I was self-aware that this behavior was present but wasn't quite understanding why. I sat with my thoughts and feelings about it. I realized it was the anxiety. I was fearful of the what-ifs.

I talked to him about what I was thinking and feeling.

"I don't want you to not go. I do want you to know what I experience when you do go and that these are my thoughts and emotions to deal with, not yours."

I wanted to make it clear to him that I will deal with the anxiety and that him knowing this information should not be a reason that he does not go and enjoy himself.

The reason I was having so much anxiety whenever he was planning to go out on the boat is because I would sit and let an entire disastrous chain of events that would lead to me losing my husband run circles around my brain. When he is out there, there's no reception so I cannot check on him to help me to feel better. Those are some long hours to leave me alone with my thinking.

It was on me to check myself, to rationalize my irrational thinking. *Girl! You are not God. These things are out of your control. His life is in His hands. He's a grown man who can handle himself, within his own control and that which he cannot control is up to God.*

I still get anxiety whenever he goes. That hasn't gone completely away. It's just not as bad because I am aware of what is going on within me and how to manage.

After I opened up to Boss about my thoughts and feelings, he began doing things that he thought might help decrease the anxiety when he goes out there on the water. He lets me know exactly where they are leaving land from right before he gets on the boat, and he messages me as soon as he has reception again. Those might seem like small unnecessary gestures, but for the anxiety they are huge and helpful.

Without self-awareness, I probably wouldn't have concluded that anxiety was pushing the agitation and snappiness. I would have blamed him for doing something to cause it. I know this because that's what I thought before I really noticed my own thoughts, feelings, and behaviors. I also was aware that I needed to work on this.

It wouldn't have been fair for me to ask him to stay home because I wanted him to avoid doing something I saw as potentially dangerous. We have been on boats together several times.

There was one unpleasant boat ride. Our friends bought a pontoon boat and invited us to go out with them. The four of us sailed out to crab island and enjoyed ourselves. We chilled on the boat and soaked in clear emerald water. We were not out there long because our friend who owned the boat had forgotten the anchor.

We headed back and made a detour to stop for gas. The waters were much choppier going back in than they were coming out. As the waves got bigger and faster, the boat rocked unsteadily. From my perception the waves were angrily bashing against the boat, clashing against its front door until it opened. Boss pushed the door against the water, closing it back each time.

Our friend was steering the boat with his best efforts. I was trying to keep my butt from sliding off the seat as we rocked side to side, forward and back. The anxiety boosted. I prayed.

A bird began to fly over us. It stayed with the boat as the waves crashed into the boat and the boat did its best to fight back. I watched the bird fly low above our heads as if it was watching over us. It stayed with us. As we got closer to our destination the waters got calmer, so did the boat and so did the anxiety. The bird flew away.

I am convinced that the bird was there as a sign that we were protected. It didn't look like a prey bird, but the only other logical reason would be that the bird was waiting for us to become its food. I believe in signs from God so I will go with my first thought.

I have accepted that I am an overthinker. Accepting it also came with understanding that I cannot allow overthinking to hold me back much less hold someone else back. Sometimes it's our intuition that helps us to make informed and safe decisions, and other times, we need to get out of our head.

Although I can take a perfectly peaceful quiet moment and mindlessly turn it into an egregious scene play, some of my overthinking is situational.

Boss, Cam and I took a quick weekend trip to Atlanta. My bestie and godson Amaryan met us there. We all left the airport together on the sky train to pick up a rental car that we shared. A couple days later, we returned to the rental car agency, dropped the car off and hopped on the sky train to head back to the airport for our departing flight back home.

If you have ever been on the sky train in Atlanta, you know that passengers hop on quickly before the doors close, and the train pulls off for a swift ride to its next brief stop. We were in the back, so I sat while Boss, Kisa, Amaryan and Cam stood next to me holding on to the handrail.

The automated safety announcement came through the speakers right before the doors closed and the train slid off quickly. It was less than a minute after departure before the train began to slow down. An automated announcement that we had arrived at our destination sounded through the speakers before the doors opened.

The door opened to nothing. Just air and opportunity to end up falling to our death if we stepped off that train. We were stopped in the middle of the track outside, fifty-seven feet in the air. No one spoke at first. We all just looked around, and I am sure I wasn't the only one wondering what in the *Final Destination* is going on.

I panicked! The guy sitting across from me pressed the help button. For about the first forty-five seconds, no one responded. It felt like forever waiting for an attendant's voice to come from the other side of the speaker. My thoughts started running a marathon in my mind. I let it all play out. This would be how my life would end. Another train would run into us and knock us off the tracks or if not, the train would somehow fall off the track on its own. Our family and friends would be devastated as they sat and watched the news reveal the details of how the Hartfield-Jackson International Airport sky train malfunctioned, falling out the tracks, smashing to the ground and killing multiple people, including me and my family.

Then the panic attack prevailed accompanied by tears, a rapid heartbeat, and my attempts to inhale slowly through the nose, exhale slowly from the mouth so I could breathe and calm myself.

They got us back on track within a matter of minutes. The rest of the short ride was slow and agonizing for me. The situation itself was scary but the overthinking caused panic.

That is what happens when we allow our minds to enter the wilderness and wander around aimlessly.

Sometimes it is not overthinking that can leave us standing in our own way. It's the underthinking as well—not thinking things through enough. It's early in life that we can start to make poor choices that can result in consequences that we could have avoided. Like the seesaw incident and how I willingly chose to try one-upping Tony by being the brave little girl that will do something her big brother refused to do. Well, unfortunately my cockiness literally resulted in a busted head.

Some poor choices I made earlier in life could have resulted in more severe consequences. So often, God covers us even when we are caught up in our own will. It was in my teenage years that I begin to discover God's grace and his mercy in my life. As I reflect as an adult, I understand his grace and mercy on a whole other level than what I did back then. Circumstances I've allowed myself in are proof of that.

One of those choices for me is in this flabbergasting story about me and Tiffany from Illinois and our dumbest shenanigans.

Tiffany and I went to visit one of my friends. We were dropped off there and decided to call my sister Angela, to come get us. Cell phones for regular-shmegular people like us, especially teenagers, were not a popular thing yet. I had a pager as the only way I could be reached when I wasn't at home. Pay phones were still scattered on just about every corner. We dropped twenty-five cents into the pay phone located right outside of the apartment complex to call her.

HEY ME! GET OUT OF MY WAY!

As we waited for my sister to come pick us up, a couple of guys rode up in a gray car. I cannot recall the exact make and model of the vehicle. They looked to be around our age. One of the guys were dark skinned and one light skinned. This is how I will identify them in the story.

"Hey, where y'all headed?" the dark-skinned guy asked.

We told them we were waiting to be picked up and that we were going to my sister's house. They offered us a ride, and we declined. They then offered to come pick us up later from my sister's house and gave us a pager number to reach them.

After we got to Angela's house, we hit them up. We gave them her address to pick us up. Angela came out to the car chatted with the guys for a few minutes and took down their license plate numbers, after asking to see the dark-skinned guy driver's license. He showed her his license. That must have satisfied her. She told us to be safe and have fun.

Boy did we go for a joyride that night. My sister lived in Mayport at the time. They drove us to the Westside, opposite the side of town my sister lived on.

On the first stop, we pulled up to a gray stucco house.

"My brother lives here. I'mma go holla at him for a second," the dark-skinned guy told us. "Y'all stay here."

We didn't think much of it. We sat in the car and waited patiently for them to return. When they returned the joyride continued.

On the second stop, he pulled up outside of an apartment complex that I was not familiar with. He parked outside of the gate in the back of the complex.

"My mama lives here. She owes me some money."

The dark-skinned dude told us, "We will be right back. Do not open this car door. If you do the alarm will go off, and we will know y'all opened it."

Me and Tiffany looked at each other. *What is this, a hostage situation?* I thought.

This ride out through the town got weird quickly and something was feeling off. After they got out and locked us in the car, we talked about our next move. We didn't know if we should get out and run for our lives or wait for them to get back.

My street smarts were not present and apparently neither were Tiffany's. We decided to wait.

They came back. The joyride continued.

As we rode around the Westside with these two strangers we began to think about the gravity of this situation. We looked at each other as if we knew what the other was thinking. She shifted in her seat. She started asking them personal questions, like she was trying to get to know them better. I sat stiff and tense.

The dark-skinned guy spoke up with a bright idea. *NOT!*

"Hey, listen, we gonna go to the carnival and we are going to distract an old lady." He continued to tell us his plan. "Then y'all are going to snatch her purse."

"Oh, heeeellllll naw! Tiffany screeched with her Milwaukee accent.

"Y'all can take us home," I demanded.

We went from feeling uncomfortable to being ready to defend our lives. I was prepared to scratch some eyeballs out. This joyride had become ominous, and we wanted no more to do with it.

"Okay, okay. Y'all wanna go home?" The dark-skinned guy said with irritation, glancing up in the rearview mirror at us.

"Yup! Take us home," Tiffany told him.

The light-skinned guy obviously was just his protégé because he just sat back and went along with whatever the dark-skinned guy said or did. He barely spoke. I was starting to wonder if he was being held captive.

I am writing this book, so obviously we made it home in one piece instead of ending up in a ditch somewhere or at the juvenile detention center for robbery or aiding and abetting.

That's not even the mind-blowing part about this story though.

HEY ME! GET OUT OF MY WAY!

About a week later, after school, my brother Tony's then-girlfriend came over to our house. She told me that she was riding with these two dudes, and she mistakenly left her bookbag in their car.

She said the police came to her house after finding her bookbag and questioned her. The car was stolen.

My eyes grew wide! I was so shocked that my body started to slightly tremble. "OMG! Girl, what is the guy's name?"

When she told me his name and described the two guys and the car, I flipped out! "OMG! OMG! You gottaw3 be kidding me."

I got Tiffany on the phone in an instant. I could not believe that she and I were literally joyriding around town in a stolen car!

Some of the choices I made earlier in my life could have changed the trajectory of my entire life. It would have been me who stood in my own way of having the fulfilling life I have now, or my path would have been totally different. If there is anyone who do not believe that God was covering me, even in my ignorance just based off this story alone I don't know how else to convince them.

I cannot even count the number of times I have had to tell myself to stop the lying.

Girl just stop it already, okay?

I have told myself on so many occasions that I am not prepared to do something that I am indeed equipped to do, that I don't have what it takes, even if it has been proven that I do. That imposter syndrome can be a beast and the biggest liar you might ever encounter.

Imposter syndrome lives in our heads. It tells us that we are not worthy of something that we deserve. It tells us that we don't know what we are doing so we aren't ready to accept a certain position. We aren't qualified to speak to hundreds or thousands of people about the thing we are great at because regardless of how awesome the work that we produce may be, we just aren't good enough.

You ever felt confident around one group of people but not so confident around another group? Maybe you were intimidated by some of the people in the group that you felt less confident around. These people might be those who you think have excessive knowledge and you may open your mouth and they find out that you don't really know anything—that you are a fraud.

That is an element of imposter syndrome.

I used to be quiet about myself and my achievements and wait for others to acknowledge them. Something became clear to me one day. I should be my biggest supporter, encourager, and cheer leader. I need to lead myself openly and with confidence. If I can't do this for myself, why should anyone else? If I don't have confidence in myself, most other people will not. Some people might very easily believe in me. Others I will have to convince by the show of my own confidence.

I have stood in my own way by staying out of the way when I didn't want to be noticed by certain people. I used to feel comfortable about opening my knowledge to those who did not know much about my field but uncomfortable with opening up professionally to people in my field who didn't know me. The imposture syndrome told me that I didn't know as much as them or that I was not on the same level as many of the other therapists I interacted with. But in reality, I was well versed in my field. I didn't know everything, but who does? I will never know everything there is to know, and neither will they. To practice, is to learn, strengthen skills, and grow.

Because of this thought process I would often second guess myself. I knew I was great at what I did. I saw that in the results and feedback I got from many of my clients. I saw that in how other therapist was interested in my feedback and consulted with me. It was proven in the way therapists and clients recommended me.

It was helpful for me to remind myself that I do not need to be perfect. It is okay to not know and find out. We can be adequately skilled and still have plenty to learn.

Imposter syndrome may tell us one thing but looking at the evidence will reveal the truth. We can allow imposter syndrome to tie us down or we can let the truth set us free.

One of my job responsibilities as a welfare transition career counselor was to create an individual responsibility plan or IRP with each client. Together, we identified short-term goals, long-term goals, and the steps it would take to meet them. We also identified barriers that might hinder them from meeting their goals and attempted to remove them.

Each step they accomplished was a progression and each one was acknowledged as a step toward their goals.

Sometimes we do not give ourselves credit for the small steps. We are so focused on the big things that we're working toward accomplishing that we don't realize that all the small steps are worth glory as well—not just in our careers but also when it comes to growth in all aspects of our lives. We need to lean into our self-compassion. We can very easily forget to give ourselves credit for the little treasures we gain along the way.

While we are reaching for the prize, we need to be careful not to leave behind the things that we will need when we get to it. Our detours and long paths may equip us with what we will need in the long term.

One of my sons was struggling with math in high school. Over the summer, I hired a tutor who I had heard great things about. At the beginning of his tutoring, he gave him an assessment, which determined exactly what was causing the challenges he was having with math.

There was a basic skill that he was missing earlier on when he began learning math, which was throwing off his ability to master math. Since we now knew what the issue was, we knew what he needed to work on in order to go further in his success in this area. He needed to go back to the basics.

He had taken math for several years and had almost reached the goal of graduation, but there was that one skill that caused so much of a challenge for him once he had gotten so far.

It is natural to want to take short cuts to reach where we want to be, but then we may not acquire everything we need to receive what we ultimately set out to achieve. Some of the things we think are small or that we think will not matter as much may essentially be critical, yet we pass over them as it is not much of importance.

The quickest way to get discouraged and lose hope is to overlook mini achievements when the one thing we hope to achieve the most is not coming fast as we would like it to come. Mini achievements are not insignificant.

When I received my AA in psychology, I knew I wasn't finished. If I wanted to meet my career goal, an associate degree was not going to be enough. But it was a step toward my long-term career goal. This achievement needed to be celebrated. However, this was not the first achievement in my plan that needed to be recognized. Before I completed this AA degree, I had to first enroll, then I had to take the classes and pass them. All of these are clap worthy, worthy of acknowledging.

I often instruct couples who come to me for therapy, to keep a relationship gratitude list. It is easy for all the things that are going wrong in the relationship to remain fresh and at the forefront of our minds. The pleasant interactions and gestures can become overshadowed by the challenges and fall between the cracks.

When progression is being made it can be difficult to see the small victories that come before your target relationship goal. This can seem like no progress is being made.

I am also intentional about practicing this in my own marriage. I will never like everything about Boss, but there are a whole lot of things I can love about him. Focusing on the things I love keeps the nagging about the things I do not like to a minimum while keeping my eyes on the prize—all his wonderfulness.

If there is something we are working on strengthening in our relationship, I need to give just as much attention to the small progress and attempts toward change than I do the pet peeves. If I give oversight to what can be considered as the small things and get discouraged and weary because I do not see any change, who is standing in my way but me?

We can be the one standing in the way of our own progress but placing the blame elsewhere. We can unfairly blame others for how we feel or for some consequences that our actions provoked.

When my children would get mad at me or Boss or both of us for issuing a consequence for their actions after they broke a rule, we reminded them that they are accountable for their actions. They would blame us in some way. Maybe we were mean or doing the most, in their minds.

They would talk about us to their friends or our family members because of course, we were wrong. How dare we impose on their freedoms after they didn't follow the rules to maintain those freedoms. How dare we take away the privilege of them going out with friends because they missed curfew. We were standing in their way of doing whatever it is that they wanted to do. We've all been children before; we know how that goes.

As adults, we still do that sometimes. We miss the mark somewhere and blame someone else.

If I had a dollar for every time I thought, I would be late because someone on the road was driving slowly and "made me" miss the light. If only I had made that one light, I would have been on time. But really, I would have been on time had I left the house earlier.

From my early to late twenties, I worked at the same mortgage company. During my eight years there, a lot of changes were made over time. I had several different supervisors throughout my time on the job. One supervisor in particular I liked very much. We had our moments where we bumped heads, but nonetheless, I liked her as a person.

I saw that she was struggling with her job responsibilities. I started helping her with some of her reports when she asked me to. The position I was in was production based. Every month our numbers were pulled. I mostly performed well and met my quota.

One of our managers walked around the floor and joked with the staff members often. He also had a sarcastic way of taking jabs at people about their numbers. One day he called me out about my numbers that were posted on the wall with everyone else's.

I defended myself. "My numbers are low because I am helping with her reports."

He looked at me confused. "Well, you need to be doing your own work."

One of the other supervisors gave me a heads up that in their meetings, my supervisor wasn't speaking up and telling the managers why my numbers were low nor was there any mention of me doing the reports.

I was a little upset about her not speaking up for me in meetings since I was helping her, but ultimately, my numbers were low because I was not doing the work. I was making a choice to help someone else and neglect my own work. I could have said no to helping her. I did blame her though.

I was upset because she didn't speak up for me, I was upset because my numbers were low, and I was upset because I felt used. I don't know if it was her intention to use me. I honestly think she was just trying to survive in her role, but too often, we might place complete blame on one or more people in a situation where we also made decisions while fully aware of the costs. I knew that helping her would negatively affect my numbers.

One of my biggest pet peeves is when someone does not take accountability. I am the queen of holding people accountable for their actions but in doing so, I want to also be able to hold myself accountable.

Social media is often the go-to for some people to air their grievances and gain an audience while doing it. I was that person before. I was so hurt and disappointed when someone that I thought I had a close enough relationship with lied to me about something I saw as important. I felt deceived. The intense feelings of betrayal I had were because this wasn't the first big lie nor was it the first shady deception.

I took to social media without using her name and blasted my distaste for the lies she had told me. She knew what she had done, so she caught on that my emotional rant was related to her actions. She in turn, got angry with me. We got into a heated argument over texting and some damaging and harsh things were said. We didn't speak for a while. Eventually, we begin making small talk here and there through messages. I apologized to her for the way that I handled my hurt and disappointment.

While I was not wrong for feeling the way that I felt, I was wrong for how I reacted. I took accountability for my reaction. She never took accountability for her lies. I didn't receive an apology, but I also was not looking for one. I was only responsible for my own behavior. I thought the right thing to do would be to take ownership for escalating the situation instead of confronting it with a sound mind.

I could have been totally justified in not ever holding another conversation with her again because of her actions, especially since she didn't take accountability for any of her wrongs after multiple offenses throughout our relationship. But that isn't what I wanted. However, nothing within me says get too cozy with her.

In a lot of situations that I have experienced, I didn't have accountability to take. Even still, I needed to check in with my emotions. I don't like to say that someone "made" me feel a certain way. I would rather say, "I feel this way because of this." I like to think that way about feelings because we can feel a certain way about a particular incident based on our own perceptions. Our feelings will always be real, but the thoughts behind them may not be factual.

I might feel neglected when Boss decides to indulge time into his own hobbies for a while, but is he really neglecting me? Is he *making* me feel neglected? I could do things to change the way that I feel. Even if that means shifting my thoughts about it instead of blaming him for how I feel.

This is not to say that people do not rightly feel neglected in their relationships at times or that their significant other is not truly neglecting their wants and needs. It's an example of how blaming your feelings on someone else could create turmoil within yourself and pour over into your relationships with other people if those feelings go unexamined.

Many people stand in their own way of having great relationships or peace in their life because they are blaming others for how they feel, and they dwell in those feelings.

Bar S hotdogs have been a running joke in our house for years. Daneisha and Boss will not ever allow me to live this life without bringing up those mixed-meat links.

HEY ME! GET OUT OF MY WAY!

For a while after Boss and I got married, I had almost the same exact grocery list that I had when I was single.

Since Boss was in Korea when the kids and I moved, he didn't know what most of the kitchen's ingredients looked like until he came home.

"What is this?" he asked, standing with the refrigerator door open. He was holding a pack of hotdogs.

"They are the hotdogs I always buy," I told him innocently.

"Bar S?" He laughed. "Don't buy these no more."

I was confused about what was wrong with the Bar S hotdogs. Me and my boys had been eating them for a long time. They were a steal—less than eighty cents per pack if I bought them from Walmart. I realized they ran about the same, if not cheaper, once I started shopping at the commissary on base.

I defended those hotdogs. Boss and Daneisha laughed.

"You can buy better hotdogs than these. You can at least get Oscar Meyers." Boss was not about to be eating any Bar S hotdogs and apparently, after that day, neither were the kids.

When Boss questioned me about those hotdogs, initially, I didn't see the problem, then I realized I was stuck. I was so used to being on a certain budget that when I had room to be flexible and grow outside of that comfort zone, I did not recognize it.

We both had our budget when we were single parents but now, we are in a two-income home. My mindset was still in single mother mode.

We can find ourselves in a place where we have the resources to grow and develop outside of our comfort zone but stay in our own way because we are keeping our minds boxed up. We aren't thinking openly. We're missing out on opportunities for more when we don't think outside the box.

I am not knocking the Bar S hotdogs, so if they are one of your family favorites that you love to pour over into your pork 'n' beans, don't stop adding them on your grocery list on account of my story. But if you are stuck in a mindset that could rob you of being set free from something that you have outgrown, get out of your way.

God had so many blessings stored up for me, but I was not ready to receive them. Where I was positioned in life was by my choices, and I knew there was more. The desire for more was there. So many prayers had gone up on my behalf. God had not forgotten. He had not left me. I just needed to move.

About twenty years ago, still married to Kelvin, I had a dream that I have never forgotten. My mom and I were standing in a room. I saw so many things in that room that were appealing to my eye. I wanted those things so badly in that dream.

Ironically, all the things I wanted but couldn't have, were baby items—toys, blankets, and a multitude of clothing in all colors. My mom told me that all these things belonged to me, but they were on layaway. It wasn't just a few items. There were a massive number of items. Everything was held up. I couldn't touch anything; all I could do was look at it.

I knew when I woke up from that dream that God had an abundance of blessings in store for me. At that time in my life, I was standing in my own way of receiving not only the things that I wanted but also the things he wanted me to have. I am not just talking about material things or just the things that feel good for my flesh. These things represented spiritual blessings as well. Every time he blows my mind, I think of that dream.

I am a living witness that God will attack our wants and needs in a way that we never imagined. God has aggressively showed up and showed out for me in a drastic way—several times. Outside of my mindset, outside of the little ounces of favor I thought was on my life.

HEY ME! GET OUT OF MY WAY!

God gave me the big head. Nobody can tell me anything less than what I know through experience about Him. I learned to be mindful about when I am blocking God. When God is saying, "Child, move out of my way," I need to move.

I often hear people say to others, "You are just where God wants you to be." I don't believe we are always where God wants us to be. At least when it comes to my own life, I know I had been in a place in my life that was not favorable to God's will for me at that time. It wasn't for any reason out of my control. It was due to me standing in my own will and in turn standing in my own way.

I was sitting at the oval shaped cherry wood kitchen table at my parents' house years ago with my face drawn into a sad frown, pouting. I felt defeated. I sat there and pondered on everything that was going wrong in my life. I left no woe unturned in my mind as I flipped through my mental book of sorrows. Nothing seemed to be working as I wanted it to.

My dad, with his dry humor, walked in. *"Get me out, Jesus. Get me ooout, get me out today,"* he sang and then broke out in a chuckle.

I glanced up at him, lip poking out even further than before. "That's not funny." I said ready to burst into tears.

He chuckled a little more before asking me what was wrong.

Most of what I was going through was a result of me holding myself back instead of leaning into the ability I had to create the changes I wanted to see. Once I decided that I was going to leave the pity party and start building my life up, things begin to fall into place. Not that I was not blessed in many ways already, but those blessings that were stored up started to release.

Wearing a thin gold chain around my neck, I danced around Auntea Debbie's living room sliding my feet over the dark hard wood floors. She pulled out her camera phone to record, and Kisa laughed and let out her usual, "*um um um*" and shook her head as I broke out into an offbeat rendition of Perri Jones' "Free," one of my signature songs.

The necklace I wore is a symbol of my freedom—the freedom to think outside the box, freedom from many things that held me bound, freedom to just be myself and bask in my release; a free bird that was once caged.

Finding my bird-and-cage necklace brought me so much joy. My friends and I were walking a strip of restaurant, stores, and entertainment when we came up on a boutique that held some nice what-nots and trinkets.

When I saw the bird-and-cage necklace hanging from a jewelry display, I knew I had to have it. The gold chain holds a bird charm that lies next to a cage charm. It cost me less than twenty dollars, but the sentimental value that it holds does not compare to its monetary value. It was a perfect representation of where I am in life—the freedom I feel. Looking back on my growth, I can see that I have come far in just my thinking alone. At some point in my life, I felt compelled to escape the core beliefs that no longer served me much purpose.

Thinking for myself has been freeing. Seeking God for myself without the pressure of thinking my relationship with him must look like what others desire it to be is freeing. Intentionally practicing self-awareness is freeing. Releasing the mindset that I must hold on to outdated and worn-out beliefs for the sake of pleasing others is freeing. Allowing love to resonate deep down in my heart and soul without carrying bitterness and resentment is freeing. Creating my own version of my best life—striving to be my best self while accepting my flaws and imperfections—is freeing.

I am walking in my freedom daily. In this freedom comes intentionality, not perfection. Freedom allowed me to write my story about some of the things that I have been set free from. I have a responsibility to myself to decide on my daily walk to not go back into that cage.

HEY ME! GET OUT OF MY WAY!

My therapist and I talked about my bird-and-cage necklace and its representation. I cannot quote her word for word but her words of wisdom to me looked like this: *If you encounter a situation that causes you to feel like you need to go back into that cage, you probably shouldn't. It's up to you to decide if you will be ok getting close enough to that cage when compromising but not so much that you end up back in it.*

I suggest the same for my readers—yes, you. Search for the things that might be keeping you bound or holding you back from thriving in every area of your life, whether it be you, things, places or people.

Whatever it is, it's up to you to say to yourself and the things that weigh you down, *SET ME FREE!*

Bird and Cage Necklace

Acknowledgments

I want to first thank the Lord for not only guiding me in my purpose but for covering me through all my crazy decisions so that I can fulfill those purposes.

To my Auntea Debbie and Aunt Juanita who are no longer with us. They inspired me to be my free self with their words of encouragement.

Thank you to my mommy for being the caring and nurturing mother who played a huge part in me becoming the woman I am today. And to my father for showing me what a kind and humble person looks like. Thank you both for being my guiding light.

I also want to thank my big sisters, Angela and Carol, for your immense presence in my life since I was knee high to a fly. And to my brother Chris, words cannot express the gigantic love and appreciation I have for our friendship.

My kiddos, I hope I am making you all as proud of me as I am of you all. Thank you for the patience you've all shown me as I figured out this parenting thing, that I still don't have figured all the way out.

Thank you to my Bestie Pooh for allowing me to talk your ears off day in and day out about the development, the ins and outs and everything else that came along with writing this book. And to my BFF, Nay, for not letting me doubt myself. Tip, one thing you are going to do is hype me up.

To my Jonesy Jones, the peanut butter to my jelly, the gas to my tank, the green to my grass and all that other corny stuff, thank you for your patience while I took all the time, I needed to get this book done. Thank you for showering me with love and peace and for supporting me big time while I catch all my dreams.

About the Author

April Jones is a marriage and family therapist, and life and relationship coach. She is married with three sons and two bonus daughters. She is a native of Jacksonville, FL.

By April Jones

Grow On:
A Spiritual and Mental
Wellness Devotional
Journal

My Bonus Mommy

When Gigi Visits

Kiaria's Birthday Surprise

If It Makes You Happy

Set Me Free:
A Journey Toward
Self-freedom

www.ingramcontent.com/pod-product-compliance
Lightning Source LLC
Chambersburg PA
CBHW032358100526
44587CB00010BA/287